BEFORE HOLLYWOOD

From **Shadow Play**
to the
Silver Screen

PAUL CLEE

CLARION BOOKS
New York

To my mother, Eileen,
for her great heart and strong spirit

Sidebar Picture Credits

The images used in the sidebars are from the following sources and
are used by permission of and through the courtesy of the copyright owners:

Louis Barendse: p. 6
British Film Institute: p. 120
Paul Clee: p. 155
Collège de France: p. 105
Bill Douglas Collection/University of Exeter: pp. 27, 141
Edison National Historic Site: p. 125
G. Finkenbeiner, Inc.: p. 43
Dr. Thomas Greenslade/Kenyon College: p. 30
Library of Congress, Prints and Photographs Division: pp. 46, 56, 72, 86, 95, 116, 160
North Carolina School of Science and Mathematics Foundation: p. 78
The Projection Box: p. 108
The Wilgus Collection: p. 9

Clarion Books
a Houghton Mifflin Company imprint
215 Park Avenue South, New York, NY 10003
Copyright © 2005 by Paul Clee

The text was set in 14-point Bulmer.

www.houghtonmifflinbooks.com

Printed in the U.S.A.

Library of Congress Cataloging-in-Publication Data
Clee, Paul.
Before Hollywood : from shadow play to the silver screen / by Paul Clee.
p. cm.
Includes bibliographical references.
ISBN 0-618-44533-1
1. Cinematography—History. 2. Cinematography—Equipment and supplies—History. I. Title.
TR848.C54 2005
778.5'09—dc22   2004023887

ISBN-13: 978-0-618-44533-2
ISBN-10: 0-618-44533-1

VB 10 9 8 7 6 5 4 3 2 1

Contents

A Beam of Light in a Darkened Room

Picture this: Thirty-some people are sitting in a darkened room. The scene is the basement lounge of the Grand Café in Paris, France. It is December 28, 1895. The people have come to experience the latest technological wonder of this amazing nineteenth century.

The spectators don't know exactly what they are going to see, but they expect to be dazzled. This is an age when new marvels seem to pop up daily. In just the last twenty years they have witnessed cities lit up by electricity, heard human voices carried along wires and machines that talk and sing, gazed at buildings that seem to scrape the sky, and much more.

Suddenly, a beam of light from behind the audience shines onto a sheet hung against the far wall. Then, to everyone's astonishment, pictures like nothing they have seen before appear on the sheet. These are not just still photographs, nor are they animated drawings. These are real people, and they are actually walking around!

The film lasts a couple of minutes and is followed by another, called *Workers Leaving the Lumière Factory*. It is the factory owned by the father of Auguste and Louis Lumière, the French brothers who made

A poster advertising Lumière films. On the screen is a boy stepping on a hose, from the film *Watering the Gardener*.

these films. The pictures are black and white and the workers move in a funny, jerky way. But still . . . pictures of real people just as they are in real life. Incredible!

Other films follow, all scenes from everyday life—*Feeding the Baby, The Sack Race,* and even a practical joke in which a boy is stepping on a garden hose, and when the gardener looks at the end of the hose to see why no water is coming out, the boy lifts his foot and the gardener gets watered.

The pictures seem so lifelike that a sequence of a train pulling into a station sends some of the spectators shrieking and ducking for cover, afraid that the train is about to come crashing into the theater.

After twenty minutes, the lights go on and the show is over. Ten short films. The first movies.

Now picture this: A small group of people sit in a darkened room near Naples, Italy. It is about three hundred years before the Lumières' Paris showing. The sun is shining outside, and a small hole in a window shade behind the spectators provides the only illumination. As sunlight passes through the hole, it forms a beam that falls on a white sheet hanging on the wall in front of the audience. To their amazement, not only do they see light cast on the sheet, they also see a detailed reproduction of the scene outside—a field, mountains, trees, a river. And most astonishing of all, the images move. Trees and grass blow in the wind, the river flows, cows graze in a field. Then, as if casually walking onstage, costumed actors enter the scene and begin performing a play, accompanied by musicians. The audience is spellbound. Everything looks so real—that is, except for the fact that it's upside down. This must be magic.

Productions like this, which included plays, mock battles, hunting scenes, banquets, and so on, were staged by an Italian scientist named Giovanni Battista della Porta (c. 1535–1615). The room he used for putting on his shows was an early form of theater called a *camera obscura,* which is Latin for "dark room." It is the term from which the modern word "camera" comes, and, in fact, the camera obscura *was* the forerunner of the modern camera.

One drawback to the camera obscura was that the hole through which the light passed inverted the image—turned it upside down. This feature caused a few problems for della Porta. Some of his guests were so frightened by the sight of people walking around upside down that they ran away screaming. Later, della Porta was charged with sorcery by Pope Paul V and hauled into court.

Both audiences, one in the sixteenth century and the other at the end of the nineteenth, were enjoying the same kind of experience we enjoy today when we watch television or go to the movies—the illusion of motion created by projected images.

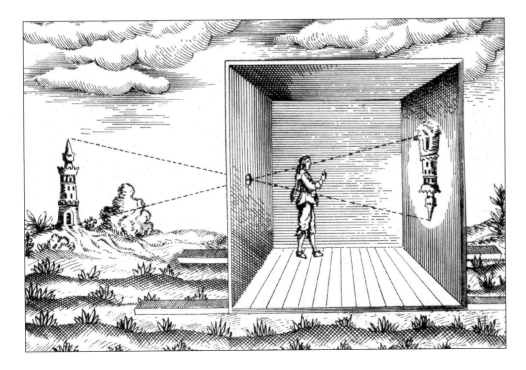

A sixteenth-century illustration of a man inside a camera obscura room. The image of the tower is projected upside down on the wall opposite the hole. THE PROJECTION BOX

In the three hundred years that separated della Porta and the Lumière brothers, the movies were born.

Louis Lumière once declared that he didn't think motion pictures had a future because people could go out on the street and see the same things. Little did he know. Within a matter of months after the Lumières' show, movie madness had swept through Europe and the United States. Theaters and opera houses were hastily converted into makeshift movie theaters, and people flocked to see whatever was offered. It didn't seem to matter what the subject of the film was; the novelty of seeing moving images taken directly from life was enough.

Moving Illusions

The fascination with moving images goes back a long way. More than two thousand years ago, the Chinese were puting on shadow plays, in which the shadows of cutout figures are projected onto a thin piece of cloth by a light from behind. The figures are manipulated like hand puppets by hidden operators while the spectators sit in front of a "screen" and watch the play unfold. This was a simple setup anyone could assemble. But in the centuries between the first shadow plays and the Lumière brothers' movies, a great deal had to be learned. It was necessary to understand how light behaves, how lenses function, and how human vision works. Inventors had to produce cameras and projectors and film. And finally, there had to be some way of recording images and making them permanent.

How did it all come together so that Auguste and Louis Lumière were able to project pictures captured from life onto the wall of the Grand Café on that day in 1895?

The Lumières' show was the culmination of hundreds of years of invention and discovery. For instance, the film they used had been introduced in 1884 by George Eastman, who had started a company in

America called Kodak. But Eastman couldn't have developed his film without the work of chemists who made better and faster light-sensitive products. The combination projector/camera the Lumières had built drew on centuries of experiments with different designs, lenses, shutters, and so on.

The story of how the simple camera obscura of della Porta evolved into the projected films of the Lumières is a fascinating tale with an equally fascinating cast of characters. Scientists, inventors, tinkerers, showmen, tricksters, scoundrels, photographers, and artists all played their parts.

There are several contenders for the title "father of motion pictures," but the fact is that no one person can lay claim to it. There are some who made bigger leaps than others, but it took hundreds of contributions over three centuries before a few minutes of film showing a train coming into a station could scare a crowd in Paris in 1895.

Oliver Sacks, a famous contemporary author and neurologist, once wrote, "It was evident that the history of science was anything but a straight and logical series, that it leapt about, split, converged, diverged, took off at tangents, repeated itself, got into jams and corners." In the same way, the road to the movies was far from a straight, smooth freeway. It was more like a country road that starts out as a path in the woods, gradually widens to a dirt road, and finally becomes a paved highway, with more and more side streets feeding into it as it goes along.

Looking back, we sometimes mistake the result of a historical movement for a goal that people living at the time were striving for. From our vantage point we can see where all the roads lead. However, most of the pioneers who traveled these roads had no idea that their work would one day contribute to making movies. They had other projects in mind, such as capturing an image on a photographic plate, advancing scientific knowledge, or developing new forms of stage productions. It was not

until the last half of the nineteenth century that making and showing movies became a deliberate aim.

PINHOLES AND DARK ROOMS

Let's start with the basics—the camera. You can't take pictures without one, and if you can't take pictures, you can't make movies. This might seem like a simpleminded question, but we can begin by asking, What is a camera?

The simplest camera is an extremely low-tech piece of equipment. You can make one by poking a tiny hole in one side of an ordinary small box. It's called a *pinhole camera,* and it really does work. You won't be photographing football games with it because the pinhole doesn't let in light fast enough to stop action. But it does a pretty good job on anything that will stay put for a few minutes in bright sun.

The earliest cameras, like Giovanni della Porta's, were really rooms, not the handheld devices we associate with the word "camera" today. If you think of a room with all the window shades pulled so that no light can come in except through a little hole in one of the shades, what you've got is a giant camera. Like della Porta's audiences, you can go inside this camera and watch the image of the scene outside projected onto the wall opposite the shade. The image is upside down but clear and in living color.

THE CAMERA OBSCURA TRANSFORMED

No one knows for sure when someone discovered that light coming through a small hole casts an image on the wall of a room, but the earliest description of an actual camera obscura is in the writings of Leonardo da Vinci (1452–1519), the Italian artist and inventor. During the sixteenth and seventeenth centuries, many improvements were made to the camera obscura. They were constructed in all shapes and sizes, from huge ones used for large-scale public shows to portable models that could be carried on one's back. Camera obscuras appeared in the form of tents and sedan chairs. The problem of the upside-down image was solved by adding lenses that would turn it right side up. This solution was first proposed by the astronomer Johannes Kepler in 1609.

A nineteenth-century postcard of children playing inside a camera obscura.

One of the first uses of the camera obscura was as an aid to drawing. A little later than Leonardo da Vinci's writing, around the middle of the sixteenth century, a man named Daniel Barbaro in Venice, Italy, described how it could be done:

Close all shutters and doors until no light enters the camera except through the lens, and opposite hold a piece of paper, which you move forward and backward until the scene appears in the sharpest detail. There on the paper you will see the whole view as it really is, with its distances, its colours and shadows and motion, the clouds, the water twinkling, the birds flying. By holding the paper steady you can trace the whole perspective with a pen, shade it and delicately colour it from nature.

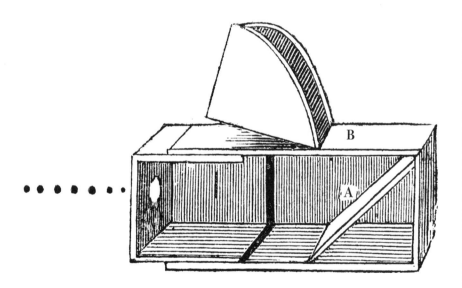
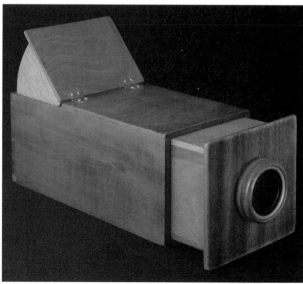

(*left*) A cutaway view of a box camera obscura. The angled mirror (A) reflects the image up to the viewing glass (B). THE WILGUS COLLECTION
(right) An English box camera obscura that can be used for drawing. It measures 9″ x 4¼″ x 4¼″. The lens is mounted in a smaller box that can be slid in and out, allowing the image to be focused. THE WILGUS COLLECTION

Better lenses were made that gave brighter, sharper images, and mechanisms were developed that enabled a lens to focus on objects at different distances from it. Some small cameras used a mirror placed inside at a 45 degree angle so that the image was reflected, right side up, onto a piece of frosted glass. A piece of paper could then be laid on the glass and the image could be traced.

These instruments were used not just as a crutch by people who couldn't draw but also by a number of well-known painters. In 1764, one writer, named Francesco Algarotti, advised in his book *Essay on Painting,* "Painters should make the same use of the Camera Obscura, which Naturalists and Astronomers make of the microscope and telescope; for all these instruments equally contribute to make known, and represent Nature."

The camera obscura came to be known as the Magic Mirror of Life. And the feeling of magic associated with the projected image has continued right up through the development of photography and motion pictures.

In the mid-1800s came the invention of photography—that is, a way to make the image captured by the camera permanent. To *fix* it, as photographers say. After that, more advanced cameras were built and new ways were discovered to record images—first on metal, then on glass, and finally on film. Materials and equipment were constantly being improved.

But the desire to create moving pictures existed long before all of these inventions were perfected. Many years before the Lumière brothers delighted Paris with their films, there were plenty of ingenious operators who used whatever means they could to create fantastic illusions in darkened rooms. ✶

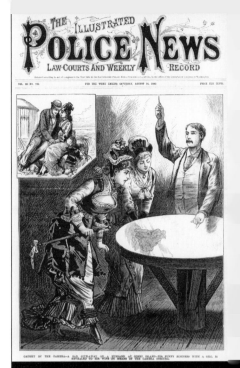

CAMERA OBSCURA ROOMS

Even though the production of visual entertainments became more and more elaborate during the eighteenth and nineteenth centuries, the *camera obscura room* remained popular. A common attraction at resorts and parks was a large camera obscura—a building, actually—that had a lens and a mirror on the roof, arranged something like a periscope, that projected an image onto a table inside. People could stand around the table and spy on whatever was going on outside, as illustrated above. These buildings continued to be constructed well into the twentieth century, and there are still quite a few of them in Britain and the United States.

··⋑ 2 ⋐··
The Magic Lantern

If you use a camera backward—shine a light from inside the camera out through the lens—what do you get? (When you think *camera* here, think big. Something at least the size of a shoe box.)

You get a simple form of a common machine: a projector. And if you put something—say, a piece of film or a glass slide with a picture on it—inside the camera between the light and the lens, you can project that picture onto a wall or screen.

At first, projectors like these were simply called lanterns. They were in use from about the middle of the seventeenth century, when lantern shows spread through the cities and towns of Europe, amazing audiences who had never seen anything like them. Today we are flooded with images everywhere we look. But when the first lantern shows appeared, photography had not yet been invented, and there was no mass production of pictures like those we see in magazines and newspapers today. There *were* paintings and handmade prints, but only the well-to-do could afford them. In the seventeenth and eighteenth centuries ordinary people saw very few pictures of any kind. The colored-

A magic lantern show given in a private home for family and friends. From the magazine *L'Optique*, 1874. LIBRARY OF CONGRESS, PRINTS AND PHOTOGRAPHS DIVISION

glass icons and wall paintings in churches and the pictures on signs advertising shops and inns were the only images most of them ever saw. Few people could afford books, and not many books contained illustrations. What's more, the high cost of paper and ink prevented most people from even making their own pictures. Children probably did their drawing in the dirt with sticks.

In a world with so few images, it's no wonder that lantern shows, with their enlarged, luminous colored picures, were such a marvel.

THE FIRST LANTERN

The invention of the projecting lantern is credited by most historians to the Dutch astronomer and inventor Christiaan Huygens (1629–1695). There are earlier references to attempts to use the camera obscura as a projector, going back to a drawing by Johannes de Fontana in 1420. But Huygens was apparently the first to put together all the elements needed to make a successful projecting lantern—a camera obscura fitted with a condensing lens, a focusing lens, and a light source amplified by a mirror.

The condensing lens, which was convex, was placed between the light source and the glass slide in order to concentrate the light on the image. The focusing lens was placed in front of the slide and projected a magnified image, which could be adjusted so that the image would be sharp at a certain distance.

Huygens was a prodigy. At the age of twenty-two he published works on geometry that caught the eye of some of the best mathematicians of the time. But Huygens's real passion was for the sciences of optics and astronomy. He built his own telescopes, cutting and polishing the lenses himself.

The science of optics—which encompasses the study and construction of lenses, telescopes, microscopes, mirrors, and projectors—was one of the consuming interests of the seventeenth century. Optical

Christiaan Huygens was born in 1629 to a well-to-do middle-class family in
The Hague, a city in Holland. He proposed the theory that light consists of waves,
rather than particles—a theory that was finally accepted over a hundred years later.

devices played a part in most scientific fields, and the century saw an incredible flowering of scientific thought and invention in Europe. It began in 1600, when Englishman William Gilbert first described an invisible power he called the "electric force." But the scientific revolution really got under way in earnest with the discoveries of two men. In Italy, Galileo Galilei put physics on solid mathematical ground, and in 1609 he built a telescope with which he observed mountains and craters on the moon and other celestial phenomena. In the same year, in Germany, Johannes Kepler published his first work on the laws of planetary motion, building on the sun-centered model of the solar system proposed in 1543 by Nicolaus Copernicus.

From that point on, new discoveries abounded. In England in 1628, William Harvey mapped the circulation of the blood. In 1637, the French mathematician and philosopher René Descartes formulated the principles of analytic geometry—applying algebra to geometric figures. Another Englishman, Robert Boyle, proposed an atomic theory of matter in the 1660s and became the father of modern chemistry. Later in the century, Isaac Newton invented calculus and published his famous laws of gravitation and three laws of motion.

Christiaan Huygens was an important part of this tremendous burst of knowledge and invention, and the first projecting lantern was a natural outgrowth of his interest in optics. Huygens's lantern no longer exists, but the evidence that it once did can be found in a letter to his family from 1659. This letter contains drawings of ten slides, which are intended, Huygens wrote, "for representation by means of convex glasses in a lantern." Photography didn't exist then, so the pictures on the glass slides were hand painted.

In addition to providing evidence for Huygens's invention, these earliest slides foreshadow one of the most popular themes in future lantern shows. On each slide is a drawing of a skeleton, and each one is slightly different. The skeleton is drawn in various poses, sometimes without a head or an arm or a leg. Huygens's idea was that by manipulating the slides in a certain way as they were projected in the lantern, he could make the skeleton fly apart, its bones scattering in all directions.

Huygens never attached much importance to his lantern, judging it to be nothing more than a trivial curiosity of no scientific or social value. But in 1658, Thomas Walgensten, a mathematician at the University of Leyden in the Netherlands, took Huygens's design, improved on it, and began commercial production of the lantern.

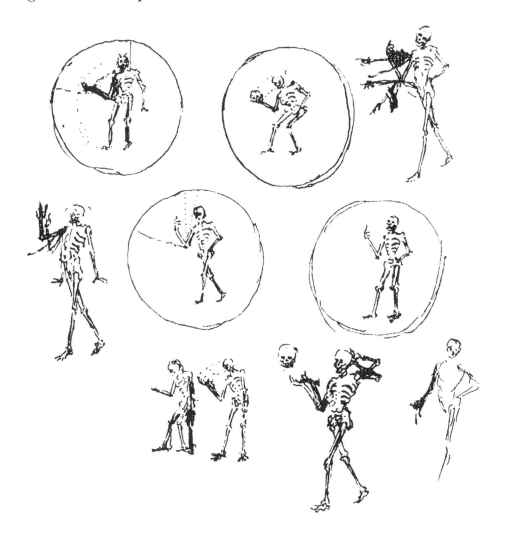

Christiaan Huygens's sketches of skeletons meant to be used as lantern slides. Collection, Visual Media— Belgium

It was only recently that Christiaan Huygens was recognized as the inventor of the magic lantern. Previously, that honor had been awarded to a German Jesuit priest and professor of mathematics named Athanasius Kircher (1601–1680), a man of many talents and wide-ranging interests.

Athanasius Kircher.

Kircher's field of study was known at the time as *natural magic,* which encompassed everything having to do with the mysterious and unexplained phenomena of nature. Natural magic didn't involve the supernatural, as the word "magic" often implied, but sought to probe the hidden forces in the world around us. It was separate from science, then known as *natural philosophy,* which dealt with what was evident to the senses.

In Kircher's time it was believed that there were mysterious invisible connections, called *sympathetic ties,* between natural objects. The phenomenon of magnetic attraction is an example of a sympathetic tie—you can't see it, but it definitely does exist. These occult, or hidden, phenomena were the subjects of natural magic, which included the field of optics.

In 1646, Kircher published an enormous ten-volume book titled *Ars magna lucis et umbrae* (The great art of light and shadow). This book is a compendium of seventeenth-century knowledge of all aspects of optics: light, shadow, lenses, mirrors, projection, illusions, and more. In his book, Kircher describes a number of optical devices and other kinds of machines he claims to have invented—and he did, in fact, invent a number of them, although some of his claims have since been proven false. His inventions included an organ that played automatically, a hydraulic clock, mechanical clocks that played music, cleverly designed fountains, and a statue that could speak and move its mouth and eyes (the voice was provided through a tube by a hidden speaker).

Among these and many more curiosities is something that looks as if it *could* be a projecting lantern. In fact, in the second edition of his opus, published in 1671, Kircher added a few pages describing a magic lantern and claimed that he had invented it. The problem was that this edition was published years after Huygens had invented his lantern. Nevertheless, for several centuries historians acclaimed Kircher as the

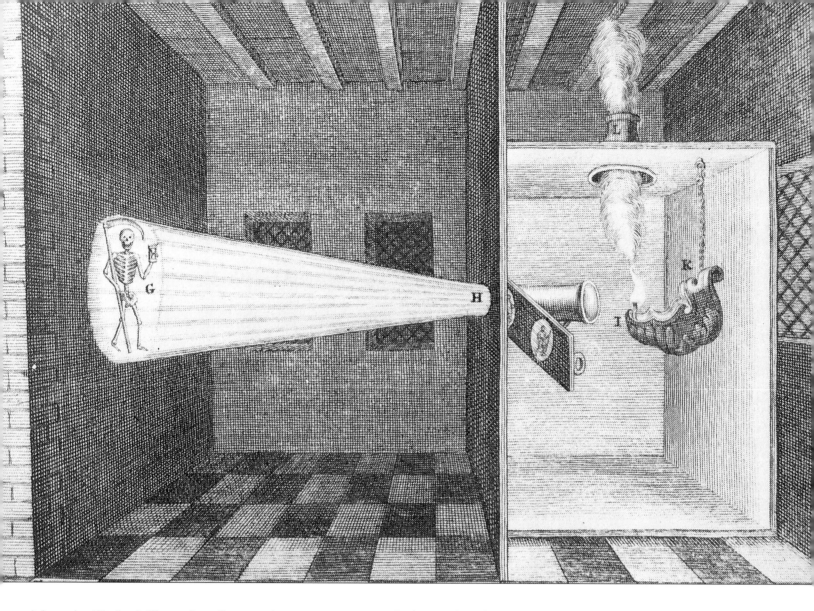

Athanasius Kircher's illustration of a projecting lantern, as it appeared in the 1671 edition of *Ars magna lucis et umbrae.* This lantern would not have worked, because the slide has been placed in front of the lens. To project a sharp image, the slide would have to be behind the lens. LIBRARY OF CONGRESS, PRINTS AND PHOTOGRAPHS DIVISION

inventor. He was dethroned only when a recent study showed that the drawing in the first edition was just a lamp that used a mirror, a candle, and a lens to throw a very bright light. But although it was not a lantern that could project images on slides, it was capable of another kind of projection. It could project words and images that were etched on the mirror itself, and Kircher still qualifies as one of the earliest producers of visual entertainments.

Kircher's technique for projecting images with his lamp originated in ancient China and Japan, where mirrors were made of bronze cast in a concave shape, something like small satellite dishes, and pictures of faces or figures or landscapes were inscribed on them with a sharp instrument. Then the surface was polished to a high shine, and when held to reflect sunlight, the mirror could project the images onto a wall. In his book, Kircher describes etching or painting images onto a mirror and coloring them with transparent paints, then using the candle in his lamp, rather than the sun, as a light source. By employing several lamps at once, fading from one to the other, he could even create a sense of movement. He also explains how to produce movement by using cutout figures.

> *Out of natural paper make effigies or images of things that you want to exhibit according to their shape, commonly their profile, so that by the use of hidden threads you can make their arms and legs go up and down and apart in whatever way you wish. With these shapes fastened on the surface of the mirror it will work as before, projecting the reflected light along with the shadow of the image in a dark place.*

Kircher even attracted flies to the surface of his mirrors and projected them, enlarged, crawling around for an even more lifelike effect.

Kircher used his lamp, which is called a *catoptric* lamp, to entertain audiences at the College of Rome, where he was a professor. "At our college," he wrote, "we are accustomed to exhibiting new pictures to the greatest wonder of the audience. Indeed, it is most worthwhile seeing, for with its aid whole satiric scenes, theatrical tragedies, and the like can be shown in a lifelike way." Even after the magic lantern proved to be a better way to tell a story using a series of images, Kircher maintained that audiences preferred the shows he gave with his lamp.

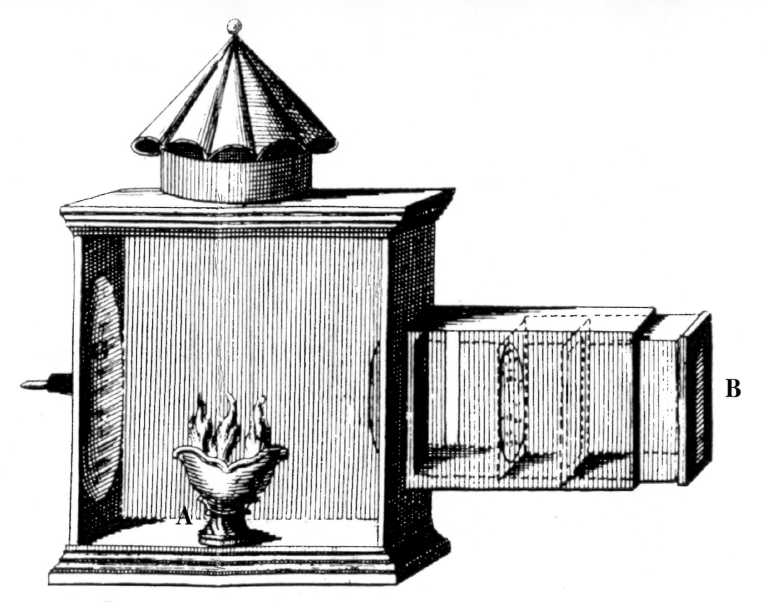

A cutaway view of a simple projecting lantern. Light is provided by an oil lamp (A). The image can be focused by moving the sliding box that contains the lens (B) in and out.

The Projection Box

Though he wasn't the first to build a magic lantern, Kircher made some important contributions to the field of optics. He added a great deal to the knowledge of how light and color and lenses behave, and he played a part in the development of the magic lantern by combining the camera obscura with mirrors. At that time, this was a necessary ingredient for making a projector because the only light sources available were candles or oil lamps, which produced a very weak light. By placing a convex mirror behind the flame, Kircher showed how the light could be amplified to throw a much brighter beam.

Another important point about Kircher's work is that it reflected the rise of a scientific, rather than a mystical, approach to nature. Kircher gave a behind-the-scenes peek at the illusions he created. He explained how he did it. This was the beginning of a centuries-long process of *demystification*—removing the mystery from natural phenomena. To all but the most sophisticated seventeenth-century viewers, there was no difference between the image of a ghost and a real one. By revealing how his apparatus worked, Kircher showed that there were natural causes behind the apparent mystery. Nevertheless, old beliefs die hard, and in spite of rational explanations, the belief that lanternists could summon spirits persisted.

THE LANTERN GOES PUBLIC

By the early 1660s, the lantern had been developed to the point that it could be used to give public shows. Miniature paintings on glass slides were projected, enlarged, onto sheets and walls, and even into smoke. The lantern show fast became one of the most popular forms of mass entertainment in Europe.

At first, these shows were private affairs given in the homes of the wealthy and the palaces of royalty. But once the craft of making lenses and lanterns became more widely practiced, traveling lanternists brought the wonder of this invention to the masses. These itinerant showmen could be found practically everywhere in Europe in the eighteenth century. They tramped from town to town, lugging their tin lanterns and slides in boxes strapped to their backs. Like any other peddlers, they walked the streets hawking their wares, stopping to give shows wherever an audience could be gathered—in barns, inns, rented rooms, and private houses. Many of these traveling lanternists

A ceramic figure of an itinerant lanternist, made in Germany. The date is unknown. BILL DOUGLAS COLLECTION/UNIVERSITY OF EXETER

were from Italy, and some historians think that their street cry of *"galante so"* (roughly translated as "fine show") gave them the name by which they became commonly known: *galanty showmen.*

Galanty shows originated as shadow plays using lanterns as the light source to cast shadows of cutout figures from behind a translucent screen. Hidden operators manipulated the figures much as puppeteers do. In fact, shadow plays were sometimes staged in outdoor puppet theaters at night after the puppet shows closed.

The shadow plays of the galanty showmen soon evolved into slide shows using the lantern as a projector. In a typical show, the pictures on the slides served as the visual framework for a narrative delivered by the showman. The subject might be a Biblical story, a newsworthy event, or just a humorous anecdote. These shows were often accompanied by music, sound effects, and even performing animals. In early illustrations, showmen are often pictured carrying a drum or a hurdy-gurdy, a stringed instrument operated by pressing keys with one hand while turning a hand crank with the other. Some lanternists also worked with assistants who played instruments during the show.

There were also lanternists who set out to educate and elevate the public with illustrated lectures. One of the earliest was a priest named Martin Martini, who had been a missionary in China. After he returned to Europe, he traveled from town to town describing his experiences in China and showing glass lantern slides he had painted himself.

The projectors these showmen used worked pretty much the same way as modern slide and movie projectors, but with a few important differences. One was that in the early days, each machine was handmade, usually of either wood or tin. Mass production hadn't yet arrived on the scene. Another major difference was the use of candles or oil lamps as a light source, and mirrors to amplify the light. And because the candles and oil lamps gave off heat and smoke, the lantern also had to be fitted

In Europe and America, shadow plays remained popular well into the twentieth century, especially as home entertainments for children. They were manufactured as kits that usually provided the figures, a small theater, a lantern, and scripts. In this nineteenth-century print, the boy with his arm behind the screen is manipulating the figures. BILL DOUGLAS COLLECTION/UNIVERSITY OF EXETER

Lanterns in the style shown were made from the eighteenth century well into the twentieth. This model, known as the Gloria lantern, is probably from the late nineteenth or early twentieth century.
NORTH CAROLINA SCHOOL OF SCIENCE AND MATHEMATICS FOUNDATION

with a chimney, such as a short piece of stovepipe. Some of the lanterns used for stage shows were so heavy and bulky they were put on wheels to make them easier to move around.

THE "MAGIC" OF THE LANTERN

Projecting lanterns soon came to be known as *magic* lanterns—and for a good reason. In a time when science was still young, anything that couldn't be explained by natural causes was generally thought to be magic. And in the minds of ordinary people, magic often meant the manipulation of supernatural forces or communication with spirits. Since hardly anyone had ever seen a projected image, and even fewer people had any inkling of how a projector worked, a magnified image suddenly springing out of thin air did indeed seem like magic. How else to explain it?

Some of the excitement and wonder of seeing a lantern show comes through in this account from 1674 by a French traveler named Charles Patin:

It seemed to me as if I had a sight of Paradise, of Hell and of wand'ring Spirits and Phantoms. . . . All these Apparitions suddenly disappear'd and gave place to Shews [shows] of another Nature. For in a moment, I saw the Air fill'd with all sorts of Birds . . . and in the twinkling of an Eye, a Country-Wedding appear'd to my view, with so natural and lively a representation that I imagin'd myself to be one of the Guests at the solemnity. Afterward, the Horizon of my sight was taken up with a Palace so stately, that nothing like it can be produc'd but in the Imagination; before which there were divers [various] Personages running at the Ring. These Heroes seem'd to be the Gods that were ador'd by Antiquity.

Magic lantern shows covered all sorts of subjects, but the kind of "magic" they were frequently associated with was "black magic." It didn't take long for unscrupulous lanternists to learn that they could easily take advantage of a gullible public. They discovered that their naive clients would plunk down good money to have the spirits of the dead "magically" raised before their dumbfounded eyes. A magic lantern could enlarge a miniature painting on a glass slide to turn it into a monstrous goblin hovering on a wall, or even in a cloud of smoke. Lantern operators would sometimes project their images directly onto tombstones and claim to be raising spirits from the grave. What a shock it must have been to people who had no concept of what a projector was, never mind how it worked. Surely it *must* have been magic.

Striking terror into the hearts of audiences was one of the earliest uses of the magic lantern, which is why it became known as the *lantern of fear*. There is some evidence that a camera obscura might have been used for this purpose as early as 1540 when, during a show in the Roman Colosseum, a magician claimed to have raised ghosts and demons from the underworld.

MAKING PICTURES MOVE

The magic lantern was capable of showing only single slides, so it was still a long way from being a movie projector. Nevertheless, lanternists and inventors like Kircher figured out ingenious ways to make images move. One way was to combine two, or sometimes three, slides. The simplest configurations, going back to Huygens's self-destructing skeleton, consisted of two painted glass slides that overlapped, one of which could be moved back and forth by hand. In this manner, a figure or object could be made to move against a stationary background. All kinds of subjects were given the illusion of movement, from light entertainments, such as a woman walking a tightrope or a gentleman losing his wig, to serious religious events, like Christ emerging from the tomb and ascending to heaven or sinners being swallowed by the terrifying, beastlike mouth of hell.

Magic lantern slides were much larger than our common 35-millimeter film. They ranged in size anywhere from three-inch squares to sheets of glass over a foot long. And until photography became a practical source of images late in the nineteenth century, all slides were hand painted. This was an art that required great care. The paintings had to be of very high quality, for all imperfections would be magnified many times when the image was projected. What's more, the paint had to have the right degree of transparency or no light would shine through, and the audience would see only a black silhouette. For this reason, most slide artists preferred watercolors to oil paints. Once the figures were painted in, the background was blackened so that the colors would stand out. Finally, a coat of clear varnish was applied to protect the painting.

During the eighteenth century, craftsmen invented many types of intricate multiple slides to create the illusion of movement on the screen. There were devices made of several overlapping sheets of glass held together in a wooden or metal frame. A different picture was painted on each slide, and the slides were set in grooves in the frame. Each slide could be raised or lowered individually by a system of levers. A levered slide of children riding a horse is described in the catalog of a nineteenth-century manufacturer, the Peck and Snyder Company: "The moving effects produced on the screen are very life-like.... The horse is put in motion by the lever, and appears to be cantering.... The children go up and down as natural as can be, and the audience can hardly believe that they are not alive."

There were also rotary slides operated by a belt drive and a hand crank. The popular "windmill with turning sails" was constructed this way. As described by its inventor, a Dutchman named Petrus van Musschenbroek in 1739, it worked like this:

> *[One slide] shows a windmill, which, with the exception of its four sails, is painted on a piece of glass, which is secured firmly against the wood without the slightest movement. The four sails are shown on another circular glass, which is glued into a copper frame which may be rotated by means of a cord, which passes around the frame and a wheel; there is a handle with which one turns it. This is the method by which one may represent a turning windmill.*

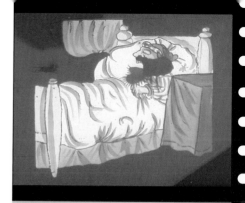

THE RATCATCHER

One favorite with nineteenth-century audiences was an animated slide called "The Ratcatcher." In it, a man was shown on his back sleeping, his jaw moving up and down. The audience would participate—as they usually did at these events—by making snoring sounds. Then suddenly a rat would appear, charge toward the man's mouth, and leap in. The audience would make gagging and choking sounds to complete the performance. In the slide pictured above, the dark spot over the bedpost at the foot of the bed is the rat heading for the sleeping man's mouth.

This projection kaleidoscope slide, also known as a Chromotrope, contains several brightly colored glass disks that turn when the handle is cranked. The slide is inserted in a lantern, and when the disks turn, a constantly changing geometric pattern is thrown against the wall. NORTH CAROLINA SCHOOL OF SCIENCE AND MATHEMATICS FOUNDATION

Other types of slides used various combinations of cogs, pulleys, and gears to create movement.

To give a panoramic view of a scene or to show a procession, long slides were used. A panorama painted on a foot-long slide slowly drawn through the lantern gave the effect of panning across the scene. According to the Peck and Snyder catalog, a procession was done this way: "A scene is painted on fixed glass, and over this is made to pass a long procession of figures—soldiers, vessels, trains of cars, caravans, as the case may be—with the most pleasing and wonderful effects."

In our age of morphing, computer-generated animation, and digitally altered photographs, it's not likely that illusions like these would fool anyone or raise suspicions of magical forces at work. But in the age of the magic lantern, they did. As Peck and Snyder explained, "It is a great mystery to the uninitiated, and they cannot understand how the transformations are made."

TECHNICAL IMPROVEMENTS

From the time of the earliest lanterns, a steady stream of technical improvements and scientific discoveries in many different fields made better and more elaborate productions possible. In optics, higher-quality glass for lenses improved the clarity of the image. One problem with the early lenses was *chromatic aberration,* the blurring of the image at the edges. This was finally solved in the mid-eighteenth century. As often happens, several people who had been working on the problem in different countries all claimed credit for the solution. This resulted in a spirited squabble and a complex court case, but it appears that the British optician John Dollond was the first to make a lens that gave a sharp image from edge to edge—an *achromatic* lens. His lens was actually composed of two lenses, one concave and one convex, sandwiched together. Each one was fashioned from a different type of glass. Dollond presented his invention to the Royal Society in London in 1758. As is usual with new products, these lenses were expensive and hard to make at first, but in time better manufacturing processes drove the price down.

Another important development was the improvement of lighting.

The earliest magic lanterns sometimes used as many as four candles or oil lamps. These lamps were fueled by an assortment of substances: olive oil, fish oil, whale oil, sesame oil, nut oils, and beeswax. But even amplified by mirrors, these light sources were too weak to throw a really bright projected image. Oil lamps were given a boost in 1784 when a Swiss chemist named Aimé Argand made one with a hollow circular wick inside a glass chimney. This slight change created a much brighter light. Argand lamps were widely used in magic lanterns in the late eighteenth and early nineteenth centuries.

But to produce a really bright image at a distance, for projection to large audiences, an even stronger light was needed.

According to legend, a Scotsman named William Murdoch discovered gas lighting one evening when he was relaxing by the fire. He put some coal dust in his pipe, then placed the pipe in the fire. The heat produced coal gas, which flamed out of the mouthpiece, burning brightly. By 1792, Murdoch had developed a system that used gas to provide light for his house.

The use of gas spread rapidly, and by the early nineteenth century most American and European cities had gaslights in buildings and along the streets. At the same time, gas became the favored fuel for magic lanterns. This gas was a refined brew of oxygen mixed with hydrogen, alcohol, or acetylene—all highly flammable. The gasses were kept under pressure in separate cylinders, then mixed together inside the lantern in a burner with a small nozzle. (A cheap version of a pressurized gas apparatus could be made by filling a large bag with gas, then placing stones on top of it to force the gas out of a small opening at the top of the bag.) The mixture of gasses was lit with a match, and the flame was aimed at a cylinder made of lime, which gave off a bright, incandescent light. This was the same limelight used to illuminate stage shows—the same light we talk about today when we say a celebrity is "in the limelight."

Gaslight worked very well in the magic lantern. It also worked very well for blowing things up. If a gas flame goes out and the gas continues to flow into the room, it's a good idea to ventilate the place before relighting. In a famous incident in a Paris theater in 1897, a projectionist disregarded this advice. He was using an oxygen-ether mixture. The flame went out. By the time he tried to relight it, the gas had spread throughout the projection booth, turning it into a bomb. The explosion killed around 140 people.

As if ghosts and demons weren't enough, attending a magic lantern show in the era of gaslight was not without its real dangers.

By the end of the eighteenth century, technical advances had opened the door to a great many new possibilities for magic lantern shows. Enterprising showmen took full advantage of the new technologies, and the shows evolved into big-time multimedia productions, full of light and sound and, most astounding of all, movement. ✳

···❧ 3 ❧···

The Lantern of Fear

In 1784, an unknown spectator wrote the following description of a *séance*—a ceremony to make contact with the spirit world:

> The supposed magician leads the group of curious persons into a room whose floor is covered by a black cloth, and in which is situated an altar painted black with two torches and a death's head, or a funerary urn. The magician traces a circle in the sand around the table or altar, and asks the spectators not to step over the circle. He begins his conjuration by reading from a book and making smoke from a resinous substance for good spirits, and from foul-smelling substances for bad ones. In a single instant the lights are extinguished by themselves, with a sharp explosive noise. At that moment the spirit called appears hovering in the air above the altar and above the death's head, in such a way that it appears to want to fly up into the air or disappear underground. The magician passes his sword through the spirit several times, which at the same time emits

This image of Robertson's phantasmagoria shows fearsome creatures being projected onto smoke. The audience members are depicted in various stages of terror, some of the men with drawn swords.
LIBRARY OF CONGRESS, PRINTS AND PHOTOGRAPHS DIVISION

a plaintive howling sound. The spirit, which appears to rise up from the death's head in a thin cloud, opens its mouth; the spectators see the mouth of the skull open and hear the words pronounced by the dead spirit, in a husky and terrible tone, when the magician asks questions of it.

During all this ceremony, flashes of lightning cross the room . . . and they hear a terrifying noise of a storm and rain beating. Shortly afterwards the torches relight themselves, while the spirit disappears, and its farewell perceptibly shakes the bodies of all members of the audience.

Séances were usually private affairs, conducted by a medium who called up shades from the spirit world. But in the late eighteenth century, showmen began putting on séances for the entertainment of the public, using the magic lantern to give the appearance that they were bringing spirits from the underworld face to face with the audience. In the above description, a hidden lantern projected the image of a spirit into smoke. Showmen loved this effect, for the ghost or goblin appeared to hang in midair right in front of the audience, and the smoke added an eerie effect. The lanternist probably used a moveable slide to make the spirit's mouth open and close.

We can also glimpse a few other tricks of the trade here. How did the lights suddenly extinguish themselves? Inside the candles there were small explosive balls, which blew up and put out the flame as it burned down. And what caused the bodies of the audience to shake at the end of the performance? It wasn't just fear and trembling or some mystical force; it was an ordinary electric shock delivered by wires hidden under the floor. There was nothing magical about these effects, but to an unwitting audience ignorant of the wonders of eighteenth-century science, magic was the only available explanation.

EIGHTEENTH-CENTURY GOTHIC

These shows played on a growing public fascination with the supernatural and the occult, a fascination that made itself evident in a variety of ways. For one, there was an upsurge of secret societies around the middle of the eighteenth century—the Rosicrucians, the Freemasons, the Illuminati, and others. These societies claimed that they could communicate with spirits, and their leaders often used magic lanterns to demonstrate their power over supernatural forces. In addition to lanterns, these men made use of an arsenal of other effects to bewitch and disorient their followers. They brewed a heady mixture of music, electric shocks, fireworks, scents, ventriloquism, and even drugs, along with other visual and aural effects.

The public preoccupation with death and the supernatural was also reflected in popular literature and drama. This was the age of the Gothic novel in England, which began with Horace Walpole's *Castle of Otronto* in 1764. The Gothic novel was full of horror, mystery, violence, and strange supernatural occurrences. It was usually set in a gloomy, isolated castle or medieval ruin, often enchanted, complete with crumbling, moss-covered walls, and riddled with secret passageways. More often than not, the plot revolved around a young heroine pursued by a forlorn villain who dabbled in the black arts. These books were designed to evoke feelings of horror in the reader. The period of the Gothic novel culminated with Mary Shelley's *Frankenstein,* published in 1818.

The magic lantern, with its ability to project ghostly images, fit in perfectly with the climate of the times.

As we know, making "spirits" appear was one of the earliest uses of the magic lantern, and over the years lanternists developed an ample stock of tricks and illusions for hoodwinking audiences. It wasn't long after Christiaan Huygens built the first working lantern in the seventeenth century that sorcerers and corrupt priests began using them as visual aids for their séances. They learned how to project their phantoms and skeletons from *behind* a screen of translucent cloth so that the spectators could not see their apparatus. They devised ways of throwing images into smoke to create the illusion of a gauzy figure hovering in the air. As one viewer described it, "That which appears extraordinary, is that the smoke does not alter the shape which is represented there, and it appears as though one could grasp it with the hand."

PHILIDOR AND HIS LANTERN ON WHEELS

Near the end of the eighteenth century, large-scale shows starring ghosts and devils and all manner of ghoulish visitors from the underworld took the art of the magic lantern to a new level. These shows were called *phantasmagoria,* from the Greek words *phantasma* (ghost or apparition) and *agora* (assembly or place for congregation).

Early lantern shows were limited in what they could do because the lanterns were fixed; once they were positioned behind the screen, they stayed in the same spot throughout the performance. A great advance in the lanternist's trade, and the advent of the true phantasmagoria, came in 1792 with the invention of the movable lantern by a shadowy character operating under the names Paul Philidor or Paul de Philipsthal. No one knows for sure who he was, but he revolutionized the art of terrorizing audiences when he put his magic lantern on wheels.

This modest innovation opened a whole new dimension of effects. Now from behind the screen, the size of the image could easily be enlarged or reduced by moving the projector back and forth. And because we tend to interpret a shrinking figure as a figure moving away, the change in size gave the illusion of movement: as the projector was pulled back from the screen, the image swelled, appearing to move toward the audience; as it was pushed forward, the image shrank, appearing to move away. The projector was also fitted with an adjustable lens so that the image could remain in focus as the lantern moved. These improvements made it possible for terrifying figures, like hooded Death brandishing his scythe or a bleeding nun, to rush at spectators as if to attack them. Just as the train in the Lumière film sent the audience scattering, so did the creatures of the phantasmagoria. A spectator at one of Philidor's productions described the scene in this way:

The hysterical scream of a few ladies in the first seats of the pit induced a cry of "lights" from their immediate friends, which it not being possible instantly to comply with, increased into an universal panic, in which the male portion of the audience, who were ludicrously the most vociferous, were actually commencing a scrambling rush to reach the doors of the exit. . . . The confusion was instantly at a height which was alarming to the stoutest; the indiscriminate rush to the doors was prevented only by the deplorable state of most of the ladies.

PHANTASMAGORIA,

THIS and every EVENING till further Notice,

AT THE

LYCEUM, STRAND.

As the Advertisement of various Exhibitions under the above Title, may possibly mislead the unsuspecting Part o. the Public (and particularly Strangers from the Country) in their Opinion of the ORIGINAL PHANTASMAGORIA, M. DE PHILIPSTHAL, the Inventor, begs Leave to state that they have no Connexion whatever with his Performances. The utmost Efforts of Imitators have not been able to produce the Effect intended; and he is too grateful for the liberal Encouragement he has received in the Metropolis, not to caution the Public against those spurious Copies, which, failing of the Perfection they assume, can only disgust and disappoint the Spectators.

M. DE PHILIPSTHAL

Will have the Honour to EXHIBIT (as usual) his

Optical Illusions and Mechanical Pieces of Art.

At the LYCEUM, and at no other Place of Exhibition in London.

SELECT PARTIES may be accommodated with a MORNING REPRESENTATION at any appointed Hour, on sending timely Notice.

To prevent Mistakes, the Public are requested to Notice, that the PHANTASMAGORIA is on the Left-hand, on the Ground Floor, and the ÆGYPTIANA on the Right-hand, up Stairs.

The OPTICAL PART of the EXHIBITION

Will introduce the PHANTOMS or APPARITIONS of the DEAD or ABSENT, in a way more completely illusive than has ever been offered to the Eye in a public Theatre, as the Objects freely originate in the Air, and unfold themselves under various Forms and Sizes, such as Imagination alone has hitherto painted them, occasionally assuming the Figure and most perfect Resemblance of the Heroes and other distinguished Characters of past and present Times.

This SPECTROLOGY, which professes to expose the Practices of artful Impostors and pretended Exorcists, and to open the Eyes of those who still foster an absurd Belief in GHOSTS or DISEMBODIED SPIRITS, will, it is presumed, afford also to the Spectator an interesting and pleasing Entertainment; and in order to render these Apparations more interesting, they will be introduced during the Progress of a tremendous Thunder Storm, accompanied with vivid Lightning, Hail, Wind, &c.

The MECHANICAL PIECES of ART

Include the following principal Objects, a more detailed Account of which will be given during their Exhibition: viz.

Two elegant ROPE DANCERS, the one, representing a Spaniard nearly Six Feet high, will display several astonishing Feats on the Rope, mark the Time of the Music with a small Whistle, smoke his Pipe, &c.—The other, called Pajazzo, being the Figure of a young sprightly Boy, will surpass the former in Skill and Agility.

The INGENIOUS SELF-DEFENDING CHEST—The superior Excellence and Utility of this Piece of Mechanism is, that the Proprietor has always a Safe-guard against Depredators; for the concealed Battery of Four Pieces of Artillery only appears and discharges itself when a Stranger tries to force open the Chest.—This has been acknowledged by several Professional Men to be a Master-piece of Mechanism, and may with equal Advantage be applied to the Protection of Property in Counting-houses, Post Chaises, &c.

The MECHANICAL PEACOCK, which so exactly imitates the Actions of that stately Bird, that it has frequently been thought Alive. It eats, drinks, &c. at command, unfold its Tail in a brilliant Circle, and in every respect seems endowed with an intuitive Power of attending to the Thoughts of the Company.

The BEAUTIFUL COSSACK, enclosed in a small Box, opens it when ordered, and presents herself to the Spectators in a black Habit; which, as soon as desired, she changes with astonishing Quickness into a most Elegant Gala Dress, compliments the Company, and dances after the Manner of the Cossacks, she will also resolve different Questions. &c, &c.

The SELF-IMPELLED WINDMILL, which is put in Motion, or stands still by the most momentary Signal from the Spectators, and in a Manner which apparently does away the Idea of all Mechanical Agency.

The whole to conclude with a superb OPTICAL and MECHANICAL FIRE-WORK, replete with a Variety of brilliant and fanciful Changes.

⁂ Doors to be opened at SEVEN o'Clock, the Commencement at EIGHT.

BOXES, 4s.—PIT, 2s.

A handbill, called a broadside, advertising Paul Philipsthal's (Philidor's) phantasmagoria at the Lyceum Theater in London. LIBRARY OF CONGRESS, PRINTS AND PHOTOGRAPHS DIVISION

To spectators at the time, these experiences were very real.

Like many other showmen, Philidor made an effort to cloak his act in the garb of a higher purpose. Like Athanasius Kircher before him, Philidor declared that the real goal of his show was to unmask those unscrupulous magicians and sorcerers who claimed that they could communicate with spirits. To do this, he would reveal their secrets and demonstrate how they produced their so-called magical effects.

Philidor's claim was in keeping with the times. The eighteenth century was a strange mixture of superstition and rationality. It was, after all, the period in Western history known as the Enlightenment, when reason and science would banish belief in ghosts and spirits. Enlightenment thinking proclaimed that science would provide a rational explanation for all phenomena. The supernatural was simply the invention of ignorant people to explain what they didn't understand, and magic was nothing more than a bag of tricks. Human reason would eventually provide all the answers, and natural causes would replace supernatural beliefs.

But by the late eighteenth century, there was a growing feeling that this way of thinking was too limited. People didn't want to believe that the supernatural was just a figment of their imagination. They wanted to believe in something larger than themselves. The world described by reason and science was a cold world governed by impersonal mechanical forces. Whatever remained of a supernatural being was reduced to the role of the watchmaker who built the machine, then stepped back out of sight and let it run by itself. Many historians see the rise of public interest in the occult and supernatural during the second half of the eighteenth century as a reaction against the cold, scientific explanations of things.

The magic lantern, with its power to both mystify and enlighten, fit perfectly into this strange mixture of reason and superstition. Lanternists took advantage of both faces of the powerful medium. Phantasmagoria showmen typically claimed to be on the side of enlightenment, but it's hard to know how sincere they were. It seems there were some who genuinely took up the cause of debunking magic and sorcery, while others were quite happy to cater to the superstitious beliefs of the audience and pocket their money.

Some lanternists announced their intentions up front, as in this playbill from 1802:

THIS SPECTROLOGY [THE SCIENTIFIC STUDY OF GHOSTS], WHICH PROFESSES TO EXPOSE THE PRACTICES OF ARTFUL IMPOSTERS AND PRETENDED EXORCISTS, AND TO OPEN THE EYES OF THOSE WHO STILL FOSTER AN ABSURD BELIEF IN GHOSTS OR DISEMBODIED SPIRITS, WILL, IT IS PRESUMED, AFFORD ALSO TO THE SPECTATOR AN INTERESTING AND PLEASING ENTERTAINMENT.

But the "entertainment" seemed so authentic that even though spectators were told the image was only an image, many of them remained convinced that it was real.

ROBERTSON'S PHANTASMAGORIAS

A few years after Philidor unveiled his phantasmagoria, a Belgian scientist and showman named Etienne-Gaspard Robert (1763–1837), who called himself Robertson, took over where Philidor left off and thoroughly outclassed him. Philidor faded from sight, while Robertson became rich and famous. Robertson took—or rather, stole—everything Philidor had done and built on it, creating more and more extravagant productions. He developed a device called a *Fantascope,* a lantern on wheels that could project not only images painted on slides but also images of solid objects. For example, a skull could be placed inside it and projected, grotesquely enlarged, onto a screen. The machine could also be fitted with lenses of different focal lengths, allowing slides and objects of varying sizes to be used. In addition, some Fantascopes had two tubes with rotating shutters (mechanical devices that quickly open and close for a certain amount of time) that made it easy to dissolve one image into another.

On December 23, 1799, Robertson staged a spectacular phantasmagoria in the abandoned convent of the Capuchins in Paris. The audience entered through a dark passageway full of strange pictures and the bones of dead monks. The passageway led to a hall where an assortment of "scientific curiosities" were displayed—novelties such as distorting mirrors, peep shows, paintings that changed as they were viewed from different angles, and a talking mirror (behind which was an assistant speaking through a tube). Next came the chamber where the phantasmagoria would be presented—a large crypt lit by a single lamp hanging from the ceiling. The walls were covered with black velvet. The audience sat facing a screen.

Robertson started off with a "scientific" lecture designed to give the impression that the show would unveil the tricks of the magician. "This is a spectacle which man can use to instruct himself in the bizarre effects of the imagination," he declared. "I speak of the terror inspired by the shadows, spirits, spells and occult work of the magician: terror that practically every man experienced in the young age of prejudice and which even a few still retain in the mature age of reason."

Then, with no warning, the room was suddenly plunged into darkness and the real show began. The audience was jolted by loud thunderclaps and bolts of lightning. A funeral bell rang, calling the dead from their graves. Then a devilish little creature appeared in midair. It zoomed toward the audience, and people shrank away in terror. Just as suddenly, it withdrew and vanished. Next, the ghosts of well-known people made their appearances—Robespierre, Voltaire, Jean-Jacques

One of the few existing Fantascopes that Robertson used in his phantasmagoria shows.
COLLECTION, VISUAL MEDIA–BELGIUM

Rousseau, and others. Bats flapped around the room, a skeleton materialized out of nowhere, and more ghosts floated in the air. People were scared out of their wits.

The show was a huge success.

Robertson accomplished these effects by using a whole bag of tricks and six assistants. First, he placed several Fantascopes behind a screen so that the images were projected toward the audience. The screen was made of cloth that had been treated with wax, which made it translucent. As Philidor had done before him, Robertson created the illusion of motion by moving his projectors back and forth. To enhance this effect, Robertson linked the wheels on the machine directly to the projector lens by means of a chain, like a bicycle chain, so that as he moved the projector the lens was automatically adjusted to stay in focus.

Robertson also filled the room with smoke and then projected images of ghosts and goblins and skeletons into it from portable magic lanterns operated by assistants hidden in the audience. By moving the lanterns around, the assistants could make these creatures come and go, appear and disappear. Other assistants with portable lanterns roamed around behind the screen, adding to the effects of the lanterns on wheels.

In addition to projected images, the phantasmagoria also included live actors, eerie music, puppets, masks, and ventriloquism—all the resources of stage and street performers. It must have been quite a show.

Sound played an important role in setting the mood of the phantasmagoria, just as it does in modern movies. The showman usually wove a fearsome tale as he introduced his menagerie of spirits and spooks, and made liberal use of strange music and sound effects, such as screams, thunderclaps, and flapping wings. But since recorded music would have to wait for Thomas Edison to invent the phonograph in 1877, the "sound track" for the phantasmagoria had to be provided by live musicians.

Ventriloquism, the art of "throwing" the voice, made its debut on the eighteenth-century stage at about the same time as the phantasmagoria, and the magic lanternists wasted no time adding it to their arsenals. It's not hard to imagine how the ability to imitate various sounds or make a voice seem to come from a ghost hovering in smoke added another dimension to a phantasmagoria show.

Robertson developed a sizeable repertoire of subjects for his productions, among them the three witches of *Macbeth,* the prophet Daniel, Mohammed overcoming the angel of death, and a macabre playlet called "Edward Young Burying His Daughter." Robertson's notes show that he developed these little dramas in considerable detail. Here, for instance, is his scenario for "The Preparation for the Sabbath" (meaning the witches' sabbath):

THE GLASS HARMONICA

The favorite instrument for providing weird music was an invention called the *glass harmonica.* It was based on a discovery made by an Irishman named Richard Puckeridge in 1743. He found that the pitch of the sound made by rubbing a wet finger around the rim of a wineglass varied according to how much liquid was in the glass. He made an instrument he called *musical glasses* by lining up a row of glasses and filling each one with a different amount of water.

In 1761, Benjamin Franklin improved on this idea. Instead of glasses, he used a set of crystal bowls, each one a little smaller than the next. The smaller the bowl, the higher the pitch. There was a hole in the bottom of each bowl, and the bowls were threaded onto a rod. A handle allowed the player to turn the whole contraption while touching the edges of the bowls to make different sounds. The music created by the glass harmonica was so spooky that it was banned in some German cities because it supposedly frightened animals, caused pregnant women to give birth prematurely, and drove people to madness. Nevertheless, a number of well-known composers, including Mozart, praised the instrument and wrote music for it.

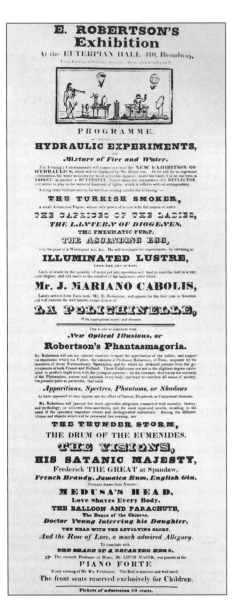

A handbill for Robertson's phantas-magoria (ca. 1825) lists the wide variety of subjects in the show. At the bottom, it is noted that music is provided by a piano forte and the front seats are reserved for children. LIBRARY OF CONGRESS, PRINTS AND PHOTOGRAPHS DIVISION

A clock strikes midnight: a witch, her nose in a book, lifts her arm three times. The moon descends, places itself in front of her, and takes on the colour of blood; the witch strikes it with her wand and cuts it into two. She starts again to lift her left hand; at the third time, cats, bats, and death's heads fly about with will o' the wisps. In the centre of a magic circle one reads the words: Départ pour le Sabbat [Departure for the Sabbath]. A woman arrives astride a broom, and many figures follow her. Two monks appear with a cross, then a hermit, to exorcize, and everything melts away.

THE SPREAD OF THE MAGIC LANTERN

Robertson's success spawned a small army of imitators and rivals. As he once remarked, "There was not a quay [pier] which did not offer you a little phantom at the end of a dark corridor, at the top of a winding stairway. The lowest amateur of physics, in every region, had his Phantasmagoria." Robertson's methods and even some of his equipment were stolen, which infuriated him and led to a court case, in 1799, in which he tried to prevent others from imitating his shows. He claimed that he was the inventor of the phantasmagoria and therefore should have exclusive rights to it. He also filed for a patent on his Fantascope, which was ultimately denied.

As it happened, the lawsuit worked against him because the court determined that it was actually Philidor, not Robertson, who had invented the phantasmagoria. Thus Robertson was portrayed as the thief, and he was further humiliated by being ordered to pay damages to one of his competitors. What's more, the court deflated the high-minded statements of the showmen when it ruled that the phantasmagorias were *not* intended to enlighten the public about the trickery of sorcerers and magicians. Instead, said the court, these shows "serve only to capture the admiration and above all the money of the public, to whom they [the showmen] are careful not to explain the causes." As a final insult, the court shattered Robertson's aspirations to scientific respectability. He argued that he had advanced the science of optics through his inventions, but the court held that this claim was false, a judgment that brought down upon him the scorn of serious scientists.

Regardless of the verdict, Robertson is now considered one of the great forerunners of the cinema. His methods were widely copied, and he developed the phantasmagoria into the true ancestor of the modern horror movie. In the eighteenth and nineteenth centuries, these productions drew large crowds all over Europe, and the shows soon migrated to the United States; the first American phantasmagoria was staged in New York in 1803, just four years after Robertson's first show in Paris. In addition to the large-scale productions in the cities, there were also touring shows that put on their own versions of phantasmagoria in local theaters and meetinghouses, and at country fairs.

Just as there is concern today about how violence in movies, on television, and in video games affects young people, the phantasmagoria raised worries in its time. In one case, in 1802, a theater operator was thrown into prison for putting on a phantasmagoria for an audience of a hundred children. The judge declared that these shows constituted a serious evil. Nevertheless, the phantasmagoria continued to be popular throughout the century.

THE TEMPLE OF SCIENCE

One of the finest magic lantern theaters of the age opened in England in 1838. It was part of the Royal Polytechnic Institution, whose purpose was to promote the wonders of science and technology to the public. Its motto was "Science for All." Magic lantern shows shared space with a hodgepodge of scientific and mechanical displays: steam engines, astronomical clocks, machines for printing paper, a diving bell, telegraphs, and so on. It

was a smorgasbord that fed a public hungry for a firsthand taste of the marvels of nineteenth-century technology.

It was fitting that the greatest magic lantern theater should be housed in the "Temple of Science." Magic and science had not yet completely parted ways, though the gap was widening. Scientists still seemed like magicians, with their ability to control natural forces and do marvelous things. At the Royal Polytechnic, a lecturer on physics might be followed by a magician on the same stage with no sense of discontinuity. And there was certainly a feeling of sorcery about the magic lantern shows.

The theater at the Polytechnic was furnished with the best equipment available, including four massive lanterns that could handle big glass slides of very high quality and project them onto a giant screen. Squads of assistants provided special light and sound effects for spectacular productions featuring subjects like the eruption of Mount Vesuvius or a voyage to the North Pole. In addition to these spectacles, each year at Christmas and Easter the theater offered new shows based on traditional stories, such as *Robinson Crusoe,* Bluebeard, *Alice in Wonderland,* and, especially at Christmastime, the stories of Charles Dickens.

One of the favorite attractions at the Polytechnic was a new kind of lantern show called the *dissolving view.* It was invented by an English theater designer named Henry Langdon Childe (1792–1874), who took the idea of multiple lantern projection a step further. He built a lantern with two lenses. With this apparatus, Childe could produce a gentle transformation from one scene to another by slowly covering the image from one of the lenses while uncovering the other, or by reducing the projection light behind one while increasing the other. In Childe's hands, winter could brighten to summer and day darken to night. His dissolving views became a fixture at the Polytechnic for many years, and were regarded as the epitome of the art.

This was just one of many improvements on the art of the projected

A nineteenth-century engraving of a lantern show using rear projection, as Robertson and Philidor would have done. The lantern shown here is an advanced model with two lenses, which would allow the showman to fade from one view to another—a technique called the *dissolve*. This technique was later adopted by filmmakers. COLLECTION, VISUAL MEDIA—BELGIUM

image that magic lanternists, artists, and craftsmen made. They created more complex slides to simulate movement. And they developed a variety of ways to use images to tell stories and create dramatic effects. Audiences, in turn, became used to the lanternist's tricks, and the terror originally inspired by the phantasmagoria was gradually replaced by a more modest thrill and an excited curiosity about how the visual effects—ancestors of today's special effects—were done. ✳

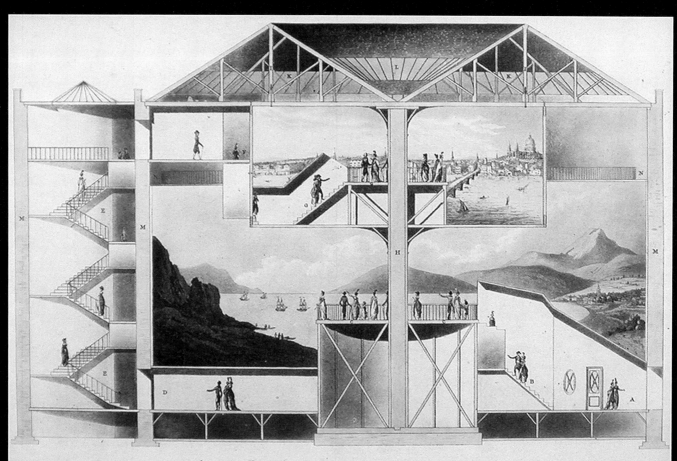

Section of the Rotunda, Leicester Square, in which is exhibited the PANORAMA.

Coupe de la Rotonde, dans laquelle, est l'exhibition du PANORAMA, Leicester Square.

Published May 16,1801.

Rob.t Mitchell Architect.

···❧ 4 ❧···
Artists of the Big Screen

The magic lantern wasn't the only show in town during the late eighteenth and early nineteenth centuries. Many new types of public entertainment emerged in Europe and North America during this time as a result of sweeping changes in the way people lived and worked. Advances in science and technology led to a new era in human history—the Industrial Revolution.

The Industrial Revolution, which began in Britain in the latter part of the eighteenth century, replaced the craftsman's hands with the machine. James Watt's improved version of the steam engine in 1769 made it possible for machines to produce goods much faster and more precisely than ever before. And there were plenty of new markets for these goods in the colonies that European powers were establishing all over the globe.

Powered by steam, factories sprang up in English towns and cities, forcing the traditional economy based on agriculture and small home-based industries to give way to the "dark, Satanic mills" of William Blake's and Charles Dickens's Victorian England. Workers who could not compete with the machines were forced to move to the growing towns and cities, where they lived in crowded tenements and labored

A postcard showing a cross section of Robert Barker's panorama, Leicester Square, London, 1789. BILL DOUGLAS COLLECTION/UNIVERSITY OF EXETER

long hours for little pay. From England the new factory system soon spread to the rest of Europe and to America.

How did the Industrial Revolution spur the growth of public entertainment? For one thing, the technology that drove industry also turned out more and better devices like magic lanterns, cameras, and light sources. But equally important, the Industrial Revolution created a middle class of merchants, manufacturers, and skilled tradespeople who found themselves with money in their pockets and time on their hands.

Throughout the nineteenth century, the middle classes—and to a lesser degree, lower-class working people as well—enjoyed a steady increase in the kinds of leisure activities that were previously available only to the upper classes, such as attending sporting events, visiting music and exhibition halls, and patronizing dramatic societies. In addition, amateur orchestras, singing groups, and a variety of local clubs and societies flourished, and new public parks, libraries, museums, and art galleries were built. Later in the century, travel by rail became wide-spread, and in summer people headed to the beaches by the trainload.

Leisure and recreation became much more a part of everyday life, and shows that featured visual entertainment of one kind or another were a vital part of it.

ROBERT BARKER'S BIG IDEA

Sometimes inspiration springs from surprising places.

In 1787, a Scottish painter named Robert Barker (1739–1806) came up with an idea for a new kind of entertainment. It happened like this:

Vacationers enjoy leisure time on the beach at Margate, England, around 1890. LIBRARY OF CONGRESS, PRINTS AND PHOTOGRAPHS DIVISION

Barker was doing jail time in Edinburgh for nonpayment of debts. One day he was sitting in his cell trying to read a letter, but the light was too dim. His cell was in the basement, lit only by a little daylight from a small opening in the ceiling near one wall. The light fell in a narrow beam on the wall just beneath the opening. So Barker held the letter up to where the light fell on the wall. He was struck by the unusual effect of the light from above falling on the letter in the darkened cell. It gave the illusion that the light was actually shining *from* the page. From this observation, Barker devised a method of painting, and of exhibiting paintings, that made him a famous and wealthy man: he combined overhead lighting with an enclosed environment and a new kind of painting.

The story goes that after his release from prison, he was climbing a hill in Edinburgh that gave a spectacular panoramic view of the whole city. He decided to make an enormous painting of the entire 360 degree view and exhibit it in a way that would capture the expansive feeling of the scene spread out before him. When he had finished the painting, he hung it inside a circular building called a *rotunda*. The canvas was large enough that it wrapped all the way around the wall, completely filling the space. The audience would view the work from inside the rotunda, as if they were standing in a huge drum with a scene painted all around the inside wall. The painting was lit dramatically from above, like the letter in Barker's jail cell, by a hidden skylight. The light that fell on the painting was the only light in the room, leaving the rest of the space, and the audience, in semidarkness. This arrangement reproduced Barker's experience in the jail: the light seemed to be shining *out of* the painting rather than falling on it.

Robert Barker had invented the first *panorama*—an unbroken view of a complete surrounding area. (The word "panorama" comes from two Greek words: *pan,* meaning "all," and *horama,* meaning "sight.")

The idea of the panorama was to create a sense of immediacy and immersion—of actually being present in the scene and enveloped by it. To make the experience as realistic as possible, panorama painters aimed at doing away with any sense of boundaries, and at reducing the feeling of distance between viewer and scene. Spectators stood on an elevated platform, close enough to the painting that they wouldn't be aware of the top or bottom—just as when you look at a real scene, you are unaware of any edges.

The panorama was a new kind of visual experience. Before actual movies, it was the first public entertainment designed to trick the eye into believing it was looking at the real thing, not just a representation. This was not the magic lantern world of ghosts and phantoms, but an attempt to reproduce the world of ordinary perception. The paintings were meticulously detailed, and artists worked out ingenious techniques of perspective to give the viewer the sensation of being in a real, three-dimensional space. The panorama was a forerunner of today's computer-generated virtual realities; its aim was to create the feeling of being transported to another place.

As "big-screen" entertainments, panoramas thrived on big subjects. Perennial favorites were battle scenes, natural disasters, major news events, cities viewed from high vantage points, and spectacular landscapes—especially of exotic foreign lands. If these elements could be combined, all the better, as in a panorama called *The Burning of Moscow* that opened in Paris in 1800. Based on one of the many fires that plagued that city during the seventeenth century, the panorama combined a view of an exotic city with a sensational disaster. It drew large crowds.

There were panoramas that would whisk you off on a virtual tour of Europe or America or the Orient, complete with the shriek of a train whistle, the rumble of a steamship engine, and the howling gale of a storm at sea. You could experience Pickett's Charge at the Battle of

Gettysburg or Lord Nelson's defeat of Napoleon's fleet at the Battle of Trafalgar. An Australian panorama artist even left transparent holes in a battle painting and set off flashes of limelight behind the screen to simulate the firing of cannon.

Subjects like these were popular not only in the panoramas but in all of the popular media that flowered during the nineteenth century, and there were plenty of them. Year by year throughout the century, especially after the introduction of photography in 1839, the production and distribution of images accelerated rapidly. Magic lanterns, photographs, exhibition halls, home entertainments, magazines and newspapers, and illustrated books all proliferated. The nineteenth century was a world transformed. Previous generations had lived in a visual wasteland, but now people's everyday lives were flooded with images. All of these media played their part in building an audience of visual consumers, so that by the time movies came along, the public was ready and eager for new visual experiences.

A few years after Robert Barker introduced the panorama, he came up with a new, improved incarnation of the rotunda. He added motion. Here's how it worked: Picture yourself sitting in the center of a large, round room. The room is sixteen feet high and forty-five feet in diameter. A light hidden in the umbrella-like roof shines against the wall. All around, the wall is painted with a series of scenes of, say, a ride in the country. Slowly, the wall turns while you and the other viewers remain stationary. As you watch, houses and shops pass by, people come and go; then the village gives way to fields with cattle grazing in the distance, workmen scything hay, a horse pulling a plow. You almost feel as if you are riding through the countryside in a carriage. This innovation brought the panorama a step closer to the experience of watching a movie. The modern IMAX, with its huge screen, is a high-tech descendant of these early attempts to provide a visual experience that envelops the audience.

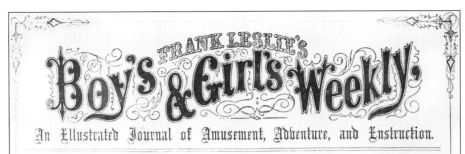

FRANK LESLIE'S Boy's & Girl's Weekly,

An Illustrated Journal of Amusement, Adventure, and Instruction.

Vol. 1.—No. 18.   NEW YORK, MARCH 2, 1867.   FIVE CENTS A COPY. $2.50 YEARLY.

DEADLY ATTACK OF A WOLF ON A MAN.

THERE is a common belief that only wild beasts of the largest and savagest kind will voluntarily attack man, except when they are in large droves. There was, however, in 1859, an instance in which a wolf attacked a farmer who was chopping wood near Lexington, Sanilac County, Michigan, and with such ferocity that, despite his utmost exertions, he was overmastered by the furious animal. It appears that early one morning the unfortunate settler was engaged in lopping some branches at a short distance from his cottage, when a wolf started from a thicket, and before the farmer could defend himself, grasped his throat with such deadly power that he dropped his ax.

His cries brought his wife to the door of the cottage; seeing the danger of her husband, the noble woman, with all that scorn of danger which distinguishes her sex when those she loves are in danger, ran to the spot, and seizing the ax, struck the wolf so well-aimed a blow, that it compelled him to release the man.

Nothing daunted, the brave woman faced the furious beast with such coolness and courage that, after a short struggle, the wolf lay dead at her feet.

The woman then turned to her husband, and vainly endeavored to stop the blood which gushed from his throat. It was all in vain, for the unhappy man breathed his last in her arms.

On examination it was found that the fangs of the monster had as completely severed his windpipe as though the throat had been cut with a razor.

RECOLLECTIONS OF MY SCHOOL-DAYS AT MAPLETON HALL.

CHAPTER V.—HOME FOR THE HOLIDAYS.

THE half-year term at Mapleton Hall ended with Christmas-tide. The last Friday before Christmas was always examination-day. The clergy and other professional men of the town and country attended in great ceremony. Many of the pupils' parents came into the town the day before and filled the Mapleton Tavern to overflowing.

The next afternoon they went away, taking their sons with them. During their stay the town was all bustle and excitement. The boys at the school had full liberty to visit their friends, and many were the happy greetings of father and son, mother and child, sister and brother.

The evening before examination-day Mrs. Milner gave a reception to the pupils and their friends. This entertainment commenced quite early in the evening, and before midnight her halls were deserted.

Frank and I expected no friends, and for that reason perhaps tried to look upon the affair with indifference. But when we heard that there was to be music and quadrilles, we relented a little. Then came the magic word "supper!"

"I ain't much of a ladies' man," said Frank, with all the indifference of a man of the world; "so it won't be worse than tooth-pulling to me to be without a partner; but when a young fellow with a healthy appetite like mine thinks of snubbing sponge-cake and sweetmeats, to say nothing of lemonade, that's what I call carrying the war into Africa. Don't you think, Wesley, we had better drop in about supper-time?"

DEADLY ATTACK OF A WOLF UPON A MAN, AND HEROIC CONDUCT OF THE MAN'S WIFE.

Illustrated newspapers and magazines, like those of the American publisher Frank Leslie, made pictures and picture stories available to everyone. Before photography, illustrations were made by engraving the image in wood or metal, then inking it and printing it in a press. LIBRARY OF CONGRESS, PRINTS AND PHOTOGRAPHS DIVISION

The panorama was so successful that within a few years Barker had built three rotunda buildings in London. Before long, special panorama houses were being constructed throughout Europe and the United States. The success of the panorama drew skilled artists to this new medium. They refined techniques for intensifying and enriching the experience. Like the magic lantern shows, the panoramas grew into multimedia productions complete with sophisticated lighting, music, narration, and sound effects.

Portable Panoramas

The panoramas shown in rotundas required large fixed buildings, so for practical purposes they were limited to cities and towns where the population was large enough to provide a steady stream of customers. But in the early nineteenth century, a new kind of panorama appeared. *Rolled* or *moving panoramas* could be moved from place to place. They consisted of a series of scenes painted on a long strip of paper or cloth that was wound on two rollers, like a scroll. As they turned, the strip passed through a frame, which usually resembled the proscenium arch of a theater, to reveal one scene at a time. These panoramas could be rolled up and carted from town to town, then set up in any theater, meeting room, school, or exhibition hall. Some of them were huge, measuring more than a thousand feet in length and standing eight to twelve feet high, and they gave an experience of virtual reality similar to the rotunda panoramas. And like the rotunda panoramas, they gave the audience the feeling of actually moving through the scene as if they were in a carriage or on a train.

The Panorama and the Armchair Traveler

The moving panorama was a natural medium for simulating the experience of travel, which became its most popular subject. The panorama came along just as nineteenth-century audiences in Europe and America were developing an intense interest in lands beyond the horizon. It was the age of empire in Europe and of frontier exploration and settlement in the United States. Travelers' tales and news reports from far-off lands piqued public interest in what these places actually looked like, and the moving panorama was perfectly suited to satisfy that curiosity. There is no accurate count of how many moving panoramas were touring Europe and America during the nineteenth century, but estimates put the number at more than a thousand, the majority of them taking audiences on virtual journeys. Like other kinds of optical shows, the moving panorama was usually accompanied by a narrator who explained the passing scene and told colorful anecdotes, as well as by sound effects like steamship whistles and the clip-clop of horses' hooves. These panoramas were the ancestors of film and television documentaries about people and places. They served as a substitute for travel for those who couldn't afford the real thing.

THE BIG SCREEN GOES TO AMERICA

The first American panorama, a copy of Robert Barker's view of London seen from the top of St. Paul's Cathedral, opened in New York City in 1795. But the first panorama by an American was created by the painter John Vanderlyn, who saw the medium as a way to introduce Americans to European culture. Like practically all American painters at the time, Vanderlyn had studied in Paris, and he was impressed by the success of the panorama there. In 1814, he made sketches of the palace and gardens at Versailles, and when he returned to his home in Kingston, New York, he painstakingly transferred the drawings to a canvas 18 feet high and 160 feet long. It took him five years to complete the work. The exhibition finally opened in a rotunda Vanderlyn had built in New York City's City Hall Park. He had great hopes, and he expected

region), and by the incident of beholding a caravan upon its line of march; a spectacle which in the remembrance always affords him the utmost pleasure. . . . Calcutta he praises also; though he has been heard to observe that the British military at that seat of Government were not as well proportioned as he could desire the soldiers of his country to be; and that the breed of horses there in use was susceptible of some improvement.

It turns out, however, that this is all a big put-on. At the end of the article Mr. Booley reveals that in all his travels, he has never left London. The most traveling he ever did was to move from one panorama theater to another.

"It is very gratifying to me," said he, "to have seen so much at my time of life, and to have acquired a knowledge of the countries I have visited, which I could not have derived from books alone. When I was a boy, such travelling would have been impossible. . . . It is a delightful characteristic of these times, that new and cheap means are continually being devised for conveying the results of actual experience to those who are unable to obtain such experiences for themselves: and to bring them within the reach of the people. . . . New worlds open out to them, beyond their little worlds, and widen their range of reflection, information, sympathy, and interest. The more man knows of man, the better for the common brotherhood among us all."

large crowds to flock to his show, as he had seen in Paris. However, the turnout was disappointing and the show was a financial failure for Vanderlyn. Apparently, Americans just didn't take to the panorama the way Europeans did. It wasn't until near mid-century that panorama fever gripped the American public.

It began in 1846, when a little-known American painter named John Banvard made the journey from Louisville, Kentucky, to Boston, Massachusetts, carrying with him a huge rolled panorama that he bragged was the longest one ever made. He claimed that it was three miles long, though its actual length turned out to be around 1,300 feet or about a quarter of a mile—still a pretty good sized piece of work. This twelve-foot-high strip of canvas took the viewer on a journey down the Mississippi River, all the way from the mouth of the Ohio River to New Orleans.

Banvard had spent a full year drifting down the river in a little skiff, camping along the riverbank, and filling a stack of sketchbooks with drawings. The journey completed, he returned to Louisville and began the four-year-long process of transferring his sketches to canvas. What he finally produced was a series of thirty-eight scenes covering the west bank of the Mississippi. Banvard's panorama met with great success in Boston and New York.

As with most productions of this kind, Banvard gave a lecture as the painted scenes rolled by. He adopted the guise of a backwoods frontiersman and spiced his talk with tales from the Wild West. After its American tour, Banvard took the show to London, where he exaggerated his frontier persona for the amusement of the English and added original music that his wife played on the piano.

Banvard followed his panorama of the Mississippi with another that was called *Panorama of the Holy Land*. This may have been the largest moving picture ever made—somewhere between twenty-five and forty-eight feet high.

ROOTS OF TODAY'S TV NEWS

The preference of today's popular media for sensational subjects has its roots in the earliest days of magic lantern and panorama shows. In addition to allowing armchair travel, moving panoramas entertained and educated audiences with recreations of historical events, tales from the Bible, and stories in the news. The natural drama of battle scenes made them a perennial favorite. Panoramas based on Biblical stories leaned toward the dramatic and catastrophic, such as the fall of Jericho or the departure of the Israelites from Egypt.

News, of course, could not be reported with the speed of a modern television camera crew. Nevertheless, panorama artists were able to give audiences a glimpse of recent events within months—a remarkable achievement, when you consider the work involved in painting such enormous canvases. It was just a scant three months after Napoleon's army set Moscow afire in 1812 that a panorama of the burning city opened in Berlin. One of the most popular panoramas, made in the 1850s by H. C. Selous, capitalized on public interest in exploration of the Arctic, a hot new topic at the time. Titled *Grand Moving Panorama of the Arctic Regions,* the painting depicted scenes from Sir James Clark Ross's attempts to find traces of the Franklin expedition, which had disappeared while searching for the North Pole.

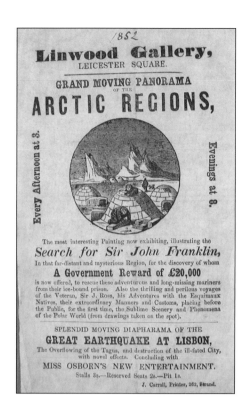

A handbill from around 1852 advertising a moving panorama show that featured the search for the Arctic explorer Sir John Franklin.
BILL DOUGLAS COLLECTION/UNIVERSITY OF EXETER

DAGUERRE'S DIORAMA

In the early nineteenth century, the magic lantern and panorama were joined by yet another form of big-screen production, one that gave audiences moving pictures with a twist. It was called the *diorama.* Today, the word "diorama" usually refers to the kind of three-dimensional display you might see in a natural history museum: stuffed animals, some plants and rocks, set against a painted background. But the dioramas that were created in the early days of this art were much more spectacular.

The first diorama was built in Paris in 1822 by the same man who, seventeen years later, would achieve fame as the inventor of the first practical process for making photographs—Louis-Jacques-Mandé Daguerre (1789–1851). Photographs made using his method were called *daguerreotypes.* Daguerre was a French artist who designed and painted sets for theaters and the Paris opera. His special talent was the creation of sensational lighting effects. Using only oil lamps, he astounded spectators with such scenes as the moon rising and a volcano erupting onstage. These effects were popular with the recently leisured middle-class audiences, who flocked to theaters offering a new kind of play called *melodrama,* which thrived on sensational effects and overblown emotions.

When Daguerre built his diorama, he designed it to make the most of the clever lighting effects he had pioneered in the theater. He started with huge pictures painted on a thin cloth called *theatrical gauze.* Like many of the panorama artists, he used a camera obscura to help make the pictures more realistic. The difference between the panorama and the diorama was that Daguerre painted both sides of the cloth. The paintings were then hung with windows behind them and skylights above, so that they could be lit from both the front and the back. The windows and skylights were equipped with screens and shutters to regulate the light, and with filters to control the color.

Lighting was the key to Daguerre's effects. By shifting the light in various ways, he could make the scene on one side of the cloth appear to dissolve into the scene on the other side. This created the impression of movement and of time passing. Simply by manipulating the light, Daguerre was able to create the illusion of clouds passing across the sun, leaves quivering in the wind, or water flowing in a stream. One of the more spectacular dioramas opened with a picturesque Alpine village. As the light changed, an avalanche roared down the mountainside and the village was swept away. Another popular *dissolve* showed a daytime view of a town gradually transformed as night fell. Because the lighting could be so precisely manipulated, the diorama could reproduce effects like a beam of sunlight shining through clouds or a sudden flash of lightning.

The diorama building consisted of a round auditorium, where an audience of about two hundred was seated, and two giant pictures, each set back about forty feet from the viewers at the end of a tunnel formed by screens. Each painting measured about forty-six feet high and seventy-two feet long. The auditorium was darkened so that looking down the tunnel to the brightly lit picture heightened the feeling of reality. The illusion was so complete that spectators sometimes threw little balls of paper at the painting, believing it was a model made of real objects.

After being seated, the audience would view one painting; then the floor would turn until it brought them around to the second one. Unlike the panoramas, these were flat paintings that displayed a single scene, or *tableau*. So instead of viewing a series of images, as in the panorama, spellbound audiences saw a scene slowly transformed into something else before their eyes.

The diorama was similar to the panorama in that it was a large-scale production that aimed to immerse the spectator in a simulation of the real world. The major difference was that the transformations of the diorama gave a sense of moving through time rather than space. Changing weather was one way of creating this effect, as shown in one reviewer's description of a diorama of Canterbury Cathedral:

The visitors, after passing through a gloomy anteroom, were ushered into a circular chamber, apparently quite dark. One or two small shrouded lamps placed on the floor served dimly to light the way to a few descending steps and the voice of an invisible guide gave direc-

tions to walk forward. The eye soon became sufficiently accustomed to the darkness to distinguish the objects around and to perceive that there were several persons seated on benches opposite an open space resembling a large window. Through the window was seen the interior of Canterbury Cathedral undergoing partial repair with the figures of two or three workmen resting from their labours. The pillars, the arches, the stone floor and steps, stained with damp, and the planks of wood strewn on the ground, all seemed to stand out in bold relief, so solidly as not to admit a doubt of their substantiality, whilst the floor extended to the distant pillars, temptingly inviting the tread of exploring footsteps. Few could be persuaded that what they saw was a mere painting on a flat surface. The impression was strengthened by perceiving the light and shadows change, as if clouds were passing over the sun, the rays of which occasionally shone through the painted windows, casting coloured shadows on the floor. Then shortly the lightness would disappear and the former gloom again obscure the objects that had been momentarily illumined. The illusion was rendered more perfect by the sensitive condition of the eye in the darkness of the surrounding chamber.

Yet More "-oramas"

The panorama and diorama were so popular that throughout the nineteenth century imitators swarmed into the business with their own versions, outdoing one another to come up with original names. There were the Pleorama, Cyclorama, Cosmorama, Kalorama, Europerama, Uranorama, and Octorama, and many others. Differences in design, some slight and some major, avoided patent infringement.

In Paris, a new slang arose based on the "-orama" craze. People would greet each other with "How's your healthorama?" or ask for a "bottleorama" of wine.

This cyclorama building in Buffalo, New York, was constructed in 1888 and designed to house a painting 50 feet high by 400 feet long. Two of the panoramas that were shown there were "The Battle of Gettysburg" and "A View of Jerusalem on the Day of the Crucifixion." At the time this photograph was taken, 1987, the building was abandoned and, as the sign announces, for lease. LIBRARY OF CONGRESS, PRINTS AND PHOTOGRAPHS DIVISION

The term "Cyclorama" caught on as the common name for panoramas exhibited in rotundas, as distinguished from rolled panoramas. Another offshoot, the Cosmorama, borrowed some effects from the diorama, but instead of using a big screen, it was set up for individual viewing through lenses set into the walls of a darkened room. The viewer would look through a lens to see a brightly lit, magnified picture at the end of a dark tunnel. Sometimes the pictures were painted on semitransparent cloth, as in the diorama, enabling one scene to be transformed into another. Like the moving panoramas for the armchair travelers, the Cosmorama promised to transport the virtual explorer to every part of the globe, as in this notice in an 1844 guidebook of London:

The Cosmorama, Regent Street, presents correct delineations of the celebrated remains of antiquity, and of the most remarkable cities and edifices in every part of the globe. The subjects are changed every two or three months; it is, altogether, a very beautiful exhibition.

Some exhibitors took their shows a step further by supplementing images with real objects and stage props. An Englishman named Albert Smith became famous for a dioramic journey of his own ascent of Mont Blanc, which opened in 1852 and ran for six years and more than two thousand performances. Smith dressed up the diorama by presenting it on a stage furnished with a model of a Swiss chalet complete with a pool and Alpine plants. His lecture was punctuated with anecdotes, songs, impersonations, and a regularly updated repertoire of references to current events. Smith also seems to have had a keen eye for the market: he produced a line of products spun off from the success of *The Ascent of Mont Blanc,* just as popular movies and TV shows today breed all kinds of related paraphernalia. Fans could buy stereoscopic photographs, plates with Smith's picture on them, magic lantern slides, and even a Mont Blanc game.

Later in the nineteenth century, one of the most successful visual extravaganzas was Poole's Myriorama. This was a family-owned travelogue that took the viewer across Europe and America, featuring large moving panoramas that employed narrative, music, sound, and dioramic lighting

The Cyclorama at Gettysburg National Military Park houses a 360 degree view of Pickett's Charge, the final Confederate attack on Union forces. The painting is 359 feet long and 27 feet high. The artist, Paul Philippoteaux, spent weeks studying the battlefield, hired a photographer to make panoramic photographs of the area, and interviewed Civil War veterans to get the details right. The work, shown here undergoing restoration, was completed in 1884. OLIN CONSERVATION, INC.

effects. The Myriorama went on the road with a staff of up to fifty, including the lecturer, musicians, machinists, and other performers. The show also included variety numbers—songs, stories, and commentary on current events—performed during the breaks between panoramas.

Assorted "-oramas" continued to multiply right up to recent times, becoming more elaborate as new techniques were devised. There was also a lot of crossover: effects developed for one medium were modified and adopted by others. For example, the moving panorama of Ross's search for the Franklin Arctic expedition used lighting effects pioneered by Daguerre, combining the movement of the rolled panorama with the shifts in time of the diorama. One scene showed Ross's ships at midnight during the Arctic summer, when the sun was still up. The ships were slowly threading their way among icebergs. A change in the lighting transformed this into a scene of ships at noon during a sunless Arctic winter, with the silvery moon casting the only illumination. This technique, similar to the dissolve employed by magic lanternists, was later adopted by filmmakers as a way of making a visual transition from one scene to another.

Without knowing it, the pioneers of these early optical shows laid much of the groundwork for the movies by developing techniques for visual storytelling and dramatic effects. By the time the Lumière brothers presented their first films, these shows had been developed to a very high level, and they remained popular well into the twentieth century. The Exposition Universelle in Paris in 1900, five years after the Lumières' first show, boasted three high-tech versions of the panorama and diorama. In one of them, visitors were treated to a forty-five-minute trip from Peking (Beijing) to Moscow on the Trans-Siberian Railway. To make the experience more authentic, the seats were built into a replica of a railway car, and since in a real railway car viewers would see objects at a distance moving more slowly than objects close by, the passing scene was made up of four different panoramas driven at varying speeds by motorized belts.

From the comfort of the railway car, travelers could move on to the deck of a ship for a sea voyage from Nice to Constantinople via another offshoot of the panorama called the Mareorama. This show consisted of two moving panoramas, 40 feet high and 2,500 feet long. The novelty of this attraction was that while these huge scrolls were being unrolled, the floor on which the spectators stood pitched and rolled like the deck of a ship at sea. To get the effect just right, the artist reportedly spent a year aboard an actual ship painting the scenes.

As full-blown multimedia spectacles, entertainments like the panorama and diorama didn't die instantly with the invention of movies. They offered experiences early films couldn't match. But they weren't able to compete for very long, as movies progressed from short snippets of everyday life to full-length feature films and documentaries. Gradually, their number dwindled, and most of the rotundas that had been thrown up for panorama shows were burned down or put to other uses. Some were converted into theaters and cinemas, while others were used as skating rinks or horseback-riding schools. But they are not all gone. There are a few that remain even today, most of them called Cycloramas, and they are still capable of working their spell on the viewers who seek them out. ✳

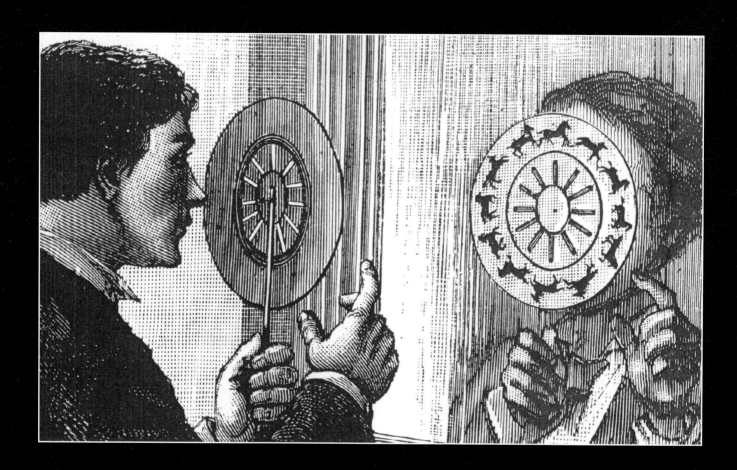

···❧ 5 ❧···

Toys to Tease the Eye

The magic lantern, the panorama, the diorama, and their offshoots whetted the public's appetite for visual entertainment, captivating audiences with their ingenious creations of virtual worlds and moving pictures. The phantasmagoria and other magic lantern shows used projectors on wheels and cleverly designed slides to make projected images seem to move. The panorama and diorama introduced the big screen and simulated the experience of movement through space and time. But scientists, inventors, and showmen still had a long way to go before a series of pictures, as on a strip of movie film, could be made to produce lifelike motion.

Around the same time that large-scale public shows were becoming popular across Europe and America, an important discovery was made that eventually supplied one of the missing pieces to the puzzle of how to make still images appear to move. It was a discovery about the way the human eye and brain work, and it led to a series of fascinating small-scale inventions that turned out to be the ancestors of the modern animated cartoon. These inventions brought a new kind of visual entertainment into the nineteenth-century home.

An engraving of a young man viewing a phenakistiscope in a mirror.
THE PROJECTION BOX

When you watch a movie, you see everything moving fluidly and naturally, just as in life. This is an illusion. If you look at a strip of movie film, you'll see that it's made up of a series of still photographs, each one slightly different from the one before it. But when the film is run through a projector at the rate of twenty-four frames per second, you're not aware that what you're looking at is a rapid sequence of photographs. You see smooth, seamless motion. Why does this happen?

For many centuries, observers noted that the eye retains images that pass before it. In ancient Greece, the philosopher Aristotle observed that when he stared at the sun, he continued to see an afterimage of it for quite some time. Leonardo da Vinci wrote in one of his notebooks that if you rapidly wave a lighted torch, "its whole course will seem a ring of flame." (You can observe this phenomenon yourself using a flashlight in a darkened room.) And you might have noticed that when you blink, everything doesn't suddenly go dark.

A few early researchers who were interested in how visual perception works tried to measure how long these afterimages remain in the eye, but it wasn't until the 1820s and '30s that serious scientific study really got under way. In 1821, a note in a British scientific journal set off a flurry of investigation. The note made an observation something like this: A person is looking through the gaps in a picket fence when a carriage with wheels made of wooden spokes goes by. What does that person see? A curious phenomenon. Instead of a rotating wheel, the viewer sees a series of *still, but curved, lines.* The spokes appear to have been frozen, their movement stopped, and their shape changed. How to explain this?

Three years later, an English mathematician named Peter Mark Roget (1779–1869) offered a solution. He attributed the effect to the ability of the retina to hold an impression of light for a certain time. This principle came to be known as the *persistence of vision*, and scientists later found that it is actually a more complicated process involving both the eye and the brain. Efforts to measure the persistence of vision produced results that varied from one-tenth of a second to one-fourteenth of a second. This phenomenon explained how the eye blends rapidly moving images together to create the illusion of continuous motion. It also led to the creation of a whole industry of curious optical devices and toys.

A SIMPLE TRICK OF THE EYE

The first of these optical toys, invented in the mid-1820s, was a simple gadget called a *thaumatrope,* a word that means "turning marvel." It consisted of nothing more than a paper disk with a different drawing on each side. When the disk was spun quickly, the two images appeared to combine to form one. The earliest example was called "The Bird in the Cage." On one side of the disk is a bird cage; on the other, a bird. Two strings are tied to holes on opposite sides of the disk. To operate the thaumatrope, you hold one set of strings in one hand and turn the disk with the other until the string is tightly twisted. Then you grasp both sets of strings and gently pull. This causes the disk to spin, and if you do it fast enough, what you'll see is a bird sitting in a cage.

Artists created many different thaumatropic disks. When this one is twirled, the flowers magically appear in the vase. NORTH CAROLINA SCHOOL OF SCIENCE AND MATHEMATICS FOUNDATION

THE ELECTRO-TACHYSCOPE

Invented by a German named Ottomar Anschütz (1846–1907), the *Electro-Tachyscope* is a spinoff of the phenakistiscope. The operator cranked the handle to turn the disk, while brief flashes of light from a *Geissler tube* illuminated the series of pictures one at a time. A Geissler tube is an early kind of gas-filled light, like a neon tube, in which an electric charge causes gas to glow.

The thaumatrope became a popular toy, and it kept many printers busy running off copies of hand-painted disks, which were packaged in small cardboard boxes. It demonstrated that the eye could form one still image from two moving ones; however, it was limited to just two pictures, and the image that appeared when the two pictures were combined did not move. Before movies could be invented, someone had to discover a way to create an illusion of motion from a *series* of still pictures.

The quest for such a device occupied some of the best minds in Europe during the early nineteenth century. The problem was finally solved by a Belgian professor named Joseph Plateau. Using an idea conceived a few years earlier by the English scientist Michael Faraday, Plateau made a flat disk, about a foot in diameter, with evenly spaced slots cut around the rim. Between the slots, Plateau drew a series of pictures of a little man dancing, each one depicting a slight advance in the dancer's movements from the one before it. The drawings were spaced at precisely the same intervals as the slots. The disk was mounted on a spindle, like a toy windmill on a stick. Grasping this device by the stick, the viewer held it up in front of a mirror and peered through the slots to see the reflected pictures. When the disk was spun, the little man in the mirror would miraculously twirl around and lift his arms and legs.

Plateau called his invention the *phenakistiscope,* which means "deceptive viewer." The principle is quite simple: the slots act as a shutter, a necessary element in creating the illusion of motion. Looking through the shutter, the viewer sees each picture on the disk for a tiny fraction of a second, which for practical purposes amounts to looking at a series of still pictures. The eye and brain of the viewer retain each image long enough to blend it with the next one into a smooth flow of movement.

Throughout the history of science, two inventors working independently have often come up with the same idea at the same time. Unaware of Plateau's work, an Austrian named Simon Stampfer was laboring on a similar device. His invention, which operated on the same principle as Plateau's, was called the *stroboscopic disk.* In 1833, Stampfer filed for a patent in Vienna and began producing these disks commercially. His customers could amuse themselves with the antics of a pair of dancers, a cyclist, a Turkish juggler, a woman operating a water pump, and a merry-go-round.

Stampfer did very well from sales of his stroboscopic disks, but Plateau never patented his phenakistiscope, and he didn't profit from it. Others, however, did. Between 1833 and 1840, the popularity of the phenakistiscope reached craze proportions. The magic wheels, as they were called, whirled endlessly in parlors and drawing rooms throughout Europe, sending dancers twirling, horses forever jumping through hoops, and wives repeatedly clubbing their worthless husbands.

These were the first toys that brought the new technology of visual imagery within reach of most middle-class families. Children could spend hours playing with a set of phenakistiscope disks, spinning them faster or slower; the phenakistiscope was the nineteenth-century version of today's video games. Even in our world of incredibly realistic computer animation, these toys hold a special enchantment for us. There is an element of fascination in them that's absent from our more sophisticated games. As you spin a phenakistiscope disk, it's as if you're getting a glimpse behind the curtain, a peek at how the whole mysterious world of movies works.

OPTICAL TOYS OF ALL SORTS

Almost all the optical inventions used in public shows found their way out of the theater or off the street and into the home. There were toy

This toy moving panorama of "The World's Wonders" includes a pamphlet with a lecture describing thirty-two places in the world that are shown on the painting. The toy is described as "Excellent for interesting children in and teaching them geography." BILL DOUGLAS COLLECTION/UNIVERSITY OF EXETER

panoramas, toy magic lanterns, and a toy called a zoetrope—a motion machine based on the same principle as the phenakistiscope.

A typical English toy panorama took you on a trip around the world by way of sights from the British Empire—Africa, India, Canada, and so on. This panorama, about three and a half inches high and nine feet long, was wound on rollers that could be turned by hand.

Another toy panorama, this one from France, simulated a ride on a train. It consisted of a paper strip with a series of paintings that looked like scenery viewed from a train window. The front of the panorama was made to look like the proscenium of a miniature theater. The audience watched as an operator behind the stage turned the rollers. On the back of the strip were notes telling about each scene, which the operator read like a tour guide.

Smaller versions of magic lanterns were also made for the home—for children as well as adults. The 1897 Sears, Roebuck catalog listed thirteen different models for children. Slide sets featured Biblical stories, folktales, Mother Goose stories, and scenes of foreign countries. There were also slides that had some educational value, featuring such things as historical events and famous people. Some lanterns were even sold with tickets and advertising posters so that children could play at putting on a real show.

In 1834, an English mathematician named William George Horner (1786–1837) invented a machine he called a *daedalum*. It was based on the same idea as the phenakistiscope, with pictures drawn between slots, but the slots were cut in a strip of paper, rather than in a disk. Then the strip of paper was wrapped around the inside of a cylinder, like a large tin can, with the pictures facing inward. Slots were cut in the cylinder to match the slots in the paper. The cylinder was placed on a round platform, something like a lazy Susan, and then spun. When the viewer looked through the spinning slots, the pictures inside seemed to move.

The advantages of the daedalum over the phenakistiscope were that no mirror was needed and more than one person at a time could view the pictures.

Strangely, Horner's invention lay dormant until 1867, when it was patented by Milton Bradley in England and William F. Lincoln in the United States. It was Lincoln who gave it the name that stuck—*zoetrope*, a word that means "wheel of life."

EMILE REYNAUD'S PRAXINOSCOPE

It seems that no sooner was one optical invention out of the box than someone started tinkering with it and came up with a flashier version. This is what happened to the zoetrope when it found its way into the hands of a young French artist named Emile Reynaud (1844–1918).

Reynaud began his career as a magic lanternist, giving illustrated lectures. He was twenty years old and already proficient in photography and the use of optical instruments when he met the famous lanternist Abbé Moigno in 1864. Moigno, who gave illustrated lectures on popular science, took the young man under his wing and taught him everything he knew about the magic lantern—from manipulating the projector and painting glass slides to the tricks of the phantasmagoria.

When Reynaud struck out on his own in 1873, he began by following Moigno's lead and giving lectures on scientific topics. But he soon branched out. He became interested in making moving images. Using the basic idea of the zoetrope, he built an optical toy called a *praxinoscope,* which he patented in 1877. Like the zoetrope, Reynaud's invention consisted of a cylinder with a series of pictures set inside, facing inward. What made it different was the use of mirrors. In the center and slightly above the cylinder was a smaller cylinder with twelve small mirrors glued to it. As the outer drum rotated, the pictures could be viewed in the mirrors. This device gave a much brighter and clearer image than the zoetrope and did

Each praxinoscope strip held twelve paintings done in bright colors on a light background. The subjects were typical of those shown in magic lantern shows and zoetropes: a juggler, a tightrope walker, a girl feeding birds, a man on a trapeze, a child playing a drum. NORTH CAROLINA SCHOOL OF SCIENCE AND MATHEMATICS FOUNDATION

away with the bother of having to peer through slots. The praxinoscope soon overshadowed the zoetrope as a popular toy.

The next year, Reynaud took his invention a step further and turned it into a miniature theater, which he called the Praxinoscope Theater. The praxinoscope was placed inside a box and viewed through an opening framed by painted curtains and decorated to look like the proscenium of a stage. Another addition was, as Reynaud explained, "a transparent mirror arranged to reflect the image of a scene placed in front of it, while allowing the figure animated by the praxinoscope to be seen through it." In other words, the animated figures could be viewed against different backgrounds. Reynaud also painted the figures on the strips against a black background so that they would be superimposed on the background scene. This was the first show of any kind to display continuous movement or to create such a flawless illusion of life.

THE PROBLEM OF PROJECTION

As entertaining as optical gadgets like the phenakistiscope and zoetrope were as toys, they were also serious scientific instruments that advanced the understanding of how we perceive objects in motion. But for more than one or two people at a time to look at these moving pictures, some way of projecting them was needed. The first attempts to build a projector were focused on adapting the magic lantern to the phenakistiscope disk. This raised several problems. Inventors soon learned that to be projected, the pictures had to be on transparent material, and a separate shutter had to be somehow incorporated into the design.

A number of machines introduced in the mid-nineteenth century succeeded, to varying degrees, in projecting images on disks. These were basically magic lanterns with the slide mechanism replaced by two disks positioned between the light source and the lens. One of the disks was transparent and contained the pictures; the other was opaque and con-

The Wheel of Life, invented by
Thomas Ross in 1869.
LIBRARY OF CONGRESS, PRINTS AND
PHOTOGRAPHS DIVISION

tained the slots. This second disk served as the shutter, allowing each picture on the disk to be projected for a fraction of a second. These disks, which were spun in opposite directions by a hand crank, had to be synchronized so that the pictures and slots intersected at just the right moment—a difficult mechanical problem.

One of the most successful projection devices was invented by a Scotsman named Thomas Ross. It was basically a magic lantern slide operated by a hand crank that turned a circular disk containing thirteen images and a slotted shutter disk that revolved in the opposite direction. He called it the Wheel of Life, borrowing the name from the zoetrope. The name stuck, and the Wheel of Life became a popular part of magic lantern shows.

The discovery of persistence of vision provided the basis for making a moving image out of a series of still pictures, and paved the way for optical toys such as the thaumatrope, phenakistiscope, and zoetrope. These ingenious toys, with their tireless jumping jacks and jugglers, made moving pictures into household entertainments. At the same time, a kind of picture never seen in the world before was stirring up a new frenzy of excitement: Louis Daguerre, inventor of the diorama, had discovered how to fix the image from a camera obscura on a metal plate. ✳

··◦ 6 ◦··
The Magic Lantern Meets the Photograph

Daguerre's process for making photographs (which he called daguerreotypes) was made public in 1839. At a joint meeting, the French Academy of Sciences and the Academy of Fine Arts voted to buy Daguerre's process and make it available to everyone. They thought that photography was too important an invention to be tied up by an individual patent.

The daguerreotype was a monumental breakthrough—pictures created by the action of light itself. Incredible! But Daguerre's method, like other early processes, was severely limited. Exposures were so long that some observers doubted that photography could ever be used for portraiture—no one could sit still for half an hour. Although improvements in the process quickly cut down the exposure time and the daguerreotype portrait business soon flourished, it would be many years before a camera could capture action as it happened. Nevertheless, the idea of moving pictures made from photographs was so compelling that a few persistent individuals refused to be deterred.

Eadweard Muybridge's zoöpraxiscope. LIBRARY OF CONGRESS, PRINTS AND PHOTOGRAPHS DIVISION

This daguerreotype of Abraham Lincoln (ca. 1846) is typical of the stiff poses that had to be held for the long exposures. The suffering sitter's neck was often placed in a clamp from behind to keep the head from moving.

THE FIRST MOVING PHOTOGRAPHS

The first moving images from photographs were achieved by painstakingly making a series of pictures. A subject was photographed once, then moved slightly and photographed again, then moved slightly more and photographed again, and again, and again, and again. The same method is still used today in certain kinds of animation, like claymation, in which a clay figure is photographed with a single-shot movie camera one frame at a time as tiny changes in position are made between frames. But in the early- to mid-nineteenth century there were no movie cameras, not even movie film, so the photographs had to be cut out, pasted on a phenakistiscope disk, and viewed in the same way as handmade images.

In spite of the limitations, though, these early experiments pointed directly to the possibility of moving pictures produced by photography. The intense interest in reproducing motion was leading some people to imagine the possibility of photographing entire scenes as they unfolded—in other words, making movies. Evidence of this appeared in a patent application filed in 1864 by a French inventor named Louis du Hauron. He described his invention as "an apparatus designed to reproduce by photography any scenes, with all the transformations undergone during a predetermined time."

Thirty years before the Lumières' show, du Hauron had a clear vision of what he wanted to do and what the technology would be able to accomplish. He foresaw in detail the coming of the movies. In his patent application he wrote:

The observer will believe that he sees only one image, which changes gradually by reason of the successive changes of form and position of the objects which occur from one picture to the other. Even supposing that there be a slight interval of time during which the same object was not shown, the persistence of the luminous impression upon the eye will fill this gap. There will be as it were a living representation of nature and the same scene will be reproduced upon the screen with the same degree of animation. . . . By means of my apparatus I am enabled especially to reproduce the passing of a procession, a review of military maneuvers, the movements of a battle, a public fête, a theatrical scene. . . .

Unfortunately, du Hauron was ahead of his time and could not make his dream a reality. The practical problem of obtaining such a rapid series of still pictures with a camera bedeviled inventors well into the 1890s.

Stereopticon shows featured dissolving views of a mixed bag of subjects for a mere dime—everything from disasters at sea to the wonders of electricity. LIBRARY OF CONGRESS, PRINTS AND PHOTOGRAPHS DIVISION

By the 1850s, photography had advanced to the point where it became possible to make photographs on glass, which could be made into slides and projected in a magic lantern. These photographic lanterns became known in America as *stereopticons*. This was a major advance over the older daguerreotype process that produced photographs on a metal plate. The appeal of images taken directly from life made stereopticon shows the latest thing, and the photograph rapidly replaced the hand-painted slide in travelogues and illustrated lectures. Though glass slides were not yet moving pictures, they were a step closer.

The first stereopticon slides were introduced in 1850 by two American brothers, William and Frederick Langenheim. In an article in *Art-Journal* in 1851, the Langenheims extolled their invention:

The new magic-lantern pictures on glass, being produced by the action of light alone on a prepared glass plate, by means of the camera obscura, must throw the old style of magic-lantern slides into the shade, and supersede them at once, on account of the greater accuracy of the smallest details which are drawn and fixed on glass from nature . . . with a fidelity truly astonishing.

A typical show consisted of a smorgasbord of photographic delights. A Langenheim show in 1852 offered a four-part program:

1. VIEWS OF NIAGARA FALLS
2. INTERESTING VIEWS OF THE UNITED STATES AND OTHER COUNTRIES OF THE WORLD
3. MICROSCOPIC VIEWS MAGNIFIED TWO THOUSAND TIMES
4. MAGICAL AND COMICAL PICTURES.

Audiences were overwhelmed by the realism of these photographs projected on a big screen. The press raved about them. A reviewer for the *New York Tribune* wrote, "The dead appear to speak; the distant to overcome space and time and be close and palpable."

At first, these shows succeeded on the strength of sheer novelty. The early ones tended to use a haphazard approach, throwing photographs together in random order. But by the 1870s, showmen had devised more sophisticated ways of presenting their work. An article in *Magic Lantern Journal* in 1875 derided "the old-fashioned, spasmodic, hitchy way of showing first a view of Paris . . . then a comic slide, and then a scripture scene, and then another Paris view, and so on." The writer recommended what he called the continuity plan—arranging slides to create the sense of a continuous story or journey.

Over time, lanternists worked out methods of visual storytelling that later evolved into editing techniques used in the movies. For example, travel shows often used such devices as dissolves from exterior to interior views, and even cut back and forth (intercuts) from, say, a traveler in a railway car to the scene outside the window. Lanternists did everything they could to make the spectators feel as if they were taking a real journey. The only thing lacking was a lifelike moving image. But work on that problem was under way.

A BET ON A HORSE

Are all four feet of a trotting horse off the ground at the same time?

According to legend, this was the question that set a California photographer named Eadweard Muybridge (1830–1904) on the path that would make him a contender for the title "the father of motion pictures."

Here's how it happened: In the 1870s horse racing was the most popular spectator sport in many parts of the United States. And as with any sport, fans were given to arguing about its fine points. One of the hot top-

The daguerreotype process produced one-of-a-kind photographs that could not be copied or projected. The search for a transparent medium was driven by the desire to make copies, as we can do from modern negatives. Celluloid film wasn't invented until the 1880s, so the first attempts to create transparent photographs centered on getting an emulsion to stick to glass.

During the 1840s, all kinds of gooey substances were tried—even snail slime. The best early results were achieved with albumen, or egg white. A little later, in 1851, an Englishman named Frederick Scott Archer came up with a better process using *collodion,* a thick gel that dries to a transparent film. It was first used in medicine to cover wounds.

The major difficulty with both albumen and collodion was that the photograph had to be taken and processed while the glass plate was still wet. This meant that the photographer had to coat the glass, expose the wet plate in

ics of 1871 and 1872 was the debate about whether all of a trotting horse's legs are ever off the ground at the same time. It was impossible to tell by just watching a horse with the naked eye. All across the country, horse racing enthusiasts took sides, and the argument boiled in the sports pages of newspapers. The story goes that a prize of $25,000 was offered to anyone who could provide solid proof to resolve the question.

This controversy caught the attention of Leland Stanford, the wealthy president of the Central Pacific Railroad and former governor of California. Stanford had taken up the breeding and racing of horses at his farm in Palo Alto. Apparently, a friend suggested he hire a photographer to try to photograph a running horse in order to settle the question.

To accomplish this task, Stanford commissioned Muybridge, who at that time was known as the best photographer on the West Coast. Muybridge had established a solid reputation as a photographer of landscapes, particularly for his views and panoramas of California. What's more, he had shown an ability to solve technical problems.

Although photography had made great strides since its introduction in 1839, this assignment was still a tremendous challenge. One problem was the low sensitivity of *emulsions,* which are made of thick substances like gelatin or albumen that are saturated with light-sensitive chemicals, then used to coat a photographic plate or film. By the 1870s, emulsions had been improved but were still much slower than modern films. Another difficulty was that cameras had no shutters. Therefore, to expose a plate, the photographer had to remove the cap from the camera lens by hand—not an easy way to catch a horse flashing by. As Muybridge explained many years later,

The problem . . . was, to obtain a sufficiently well-developed and contrasted image on a wet collodion plate, after an exposure of so brief a duration that a horse's foot, moving with a velocity of more than

thirty yards in a second of time, should be photographed with its out-lines practically sharp.

In those days the rapid dry process—by the use of which such an operation is now easily accomplished—had not been discovered. Every photographer was, in a great measure, his own chemist; he prepared his own dipping baths, made his own collodion, coated and developed his own plates, and frequently manufactured the chemicals necessary for his work. All this involved a vast amount of tedious and careful manipulation from which the present generation is, happily, relieved.

Even though Muybridge was an accomplished photographer, capturing an image of a horse that could run a mile in just over two minutes would stretch his ingenuity to the limit. When first presented with Stanford's proposition, Muybridge said he thought it would be impossible to do. But Stanford would pay well, so Muybridge decided to give it a try.

Leland Stanford was not only interested in the question of whether a running horse's feet were off the ground, he was also interested in improving his horses' performance. He thought that photographs showing exactly how horses ran would help him discover better ways of training them. One of the horses Stanford had trained, Occident, had become nationally famous, so Stanford proposed that Muybridge use Occident for his experiments. Occident was a *trotter*—a racehorse that pulled a two-wheeled buggy called a *sulky*.

TRIAL RUNS

The first attempt to photograph Occident was made in Sacramento, California, in 1872 or 1873—the date is uncertain. An article in the San Francisco newspaper *Alta California* on April 7, 1873, described how Muybridge went about solving the problem of stopping motion with his

the camera, and then develop the image immediately. Thus photographers in the field had to take a complete darkroom with them, usually packed on the backs of mules or hauled in wagons. It was a difficult, tricky business but a great advance over any other method.

The illustration on the previous page shows a photographic van used by the British photographer Roger Fenton, one of the earliest "war photographers." Fenton documented the Crimean War in 1855, using the then new *wet-plate process*. He managed to make 360 photographs working with a difficult process under terrible conditions of extreme heat and dust—not to mention warfare. Some of the finest photographs of the nineteenth century were made using the wet-plate process.

camera. First, he collected all the bedsheets he could find in the neighbor-hood and strung them up along one side of the racetrack. The idea was that the white background of sheets would reflect more light, which would make the image of the horse running in front of them stand out more clear-ly. In the first few trials, Muybridge quickly removed and replaced the cap

This photograph of Eadweard Muybridge was taken about twenty years after his experiments with **Occident.** LIBRARY OF CONGRESS, PRINTS AND PHOTOGRAPHS DIVISION

on the camera lens as the horse passed in front of him, but he wasn't able to do it fast enough. The best he could do was catch a blurry shadow.

Muybridge realized that to expose the plate quickly enough to catch an image of the horse he would need some kind of shutter. Modern shutters are built into cameras, and they can open and close in a tiny fraction of a second—fast enough in some cameras to photograph a bullet in flight. But in Muybridge's day, cameras didn't come with shutters, so the photographer had to make his own. Here is how the newspaper article described Muybridge's solution:

On the third day, Mr. Muybridge, having studied the matter thoroughly, contrived to have two boards slip past each other by touching a spring and in so doing to leave an eighth of an inch opening for the five-hundredth part of a second, as the horse passed, and by an arrangement of double lenses, crossed, secured a negative that shows "Occident" in full motion—a perfect likeness of the celebrated horse.

Muybridge placed his wooden shutter in front of the camera, which prevented light from entering the lens until the slit passed in front of it, exposing the plate for 1/500 of a second.

THE QUESTION ANSWERED

The picture of Occident running settled once and for all the question that started it: the image was faint, but the horse was clearly shown with all four of its feet off the ground at the same time. More important, Muybridge's success led to further experiments and improvements in photographic technique.

Leland Stanford was interested in obtaining more detailed information about exactly how horses run. For example, he wanted to know whether the horse's front legs are perfectly straight at the moment the feet touch the ground, or whether the heels come in contact with the ground first. He wanted to find out what variations there were in the way different horses moved.

In 1877, Stanford once again asked Muybridge to come to Sacramento to photograph Occident. Muybridge had made some technical improvements since his earlier attempts and was able to produce much better pictures of the horse. The San Francisco newspapers raved about these photographs.

Muybridge had conducted many experiments with different chemicals and had developed a process for making emulsions that enabled him to expose the plate for only $\frac{1}{1000}$ of a second. What's more, there is evidence that he used an electrical device to trigger the shutter, which was set off automatically as the horse passed in front of the camera.

The Horse in Motion

The success of their efforts spurred Stanford and Muybridge on to attempt a much more complicated project. They wanted to produce a complete study of the horse in motion. Stanford's scheme was based on an idea first suggested by the Swedish photographer Oscar Rejlander. In the early 1870s, Rejlander had written an article in which he proposed using a battery of cameras to take a series of pictures of a trotting horse.

Stanford ordered twelve special cameras fitted with shutters designed by Muybridge and constructed by Arthur Brown of Stanford's Central Pacific Railroad. Muybridge also devised an improved electrical apparatus that would fire the shutters automatically, which he claimed would expose the plate for "less than the two-thousandth part of a second."

The project was undertaken at Stanford's farm in Palo Alto. A long whitewashed shed was built along one side of the training track to house the cameras. They were placed twenty-one inches apart. Since the plates would be exposed so briefly, Muybridge needed all the light

Muybridge's layout for photographing running horses at Palo Alto, California, 1876–79. In the foreground are the wires over which the wheels of the sulky would pass. In the background is the shed, with its battery of cameras numbered one through twenty-four. LIBRARY OF CONGRESS, PRINTS AND PHOTOGRAPHS DIVISION

he could get, so the cameras were aimed across the track toward a fifteen-foot-high fence that had been hung with white sheets. Powdered lime was spread on the track to reflect even more light. Twelve sections were marked off on the sheets at twenty-one-inch intervals, and each section was numbered so that it would be easy to tell which camera had taken which picture. From each shutter a wire was stretched across the track, so that when the metal rims of the sulky's wheels crossed the wire, the shutter would be triggered.

With everything in place, Leland Stanford's master trainer, Charles Marvin, mounted the sulky and drove the horse, Abe Edgington, down the track. The *Pacific Rural Press* newspaper reported the event on June 22, 1878:

[Abe Edgington] came down the track in splendid style, with a good, square motion and firm trot. As soon as the wheel struck wire No. 1,

Camera No. 1 was closed by the means described, and the first picture taken; when it struck No. 2, the second camera had the second picture, and so on until 12 pictures were taken 21 inches apart. . . . The sound of the slides closing was like a continuous roll, so quickly was the feat accomplished.

The process was repeated with a horse and rider. As there were no sulky wheels to set off the shutters, strings were stretched across the track so that when the horse broke them the shutters were triggered. In both cases, the results were, in the words of one reporter, "a brilliant success."

Motion Pictures

From 1878 until 1881, Stanford and Muybridge continued their experiments. The number of cameras was increased from twelve to twenty-four, and the project was expanded to include other animals. Studies were made of the ox, dog, bull, cow, deer, goat, and boar. During this time, Muybridge also made his first photographs of people in motion. He photographed athletes from the Olympic Club in San Francisco performing various movements: boxing, wrestling, fencing, jumping, and tumbling.

These studies were more than interesting curiosities. Freezing the subjects in various positions enabled scientists and artists to understand in great detail exactly how they moved. When an article about Muybridge's work appeared in the French journal *La Nature* in 1878, the French scientist Etienne-Jules Marey wrote a letter to the editor praising his achievement:

What beautiful zoetropes he [Muybridge] could give us, and we could perfectly see the true movements of all imaginable animals. It would be animated zoology. So far as artists are concerned, it would create a revolution, since we could furnish them the true attributes of

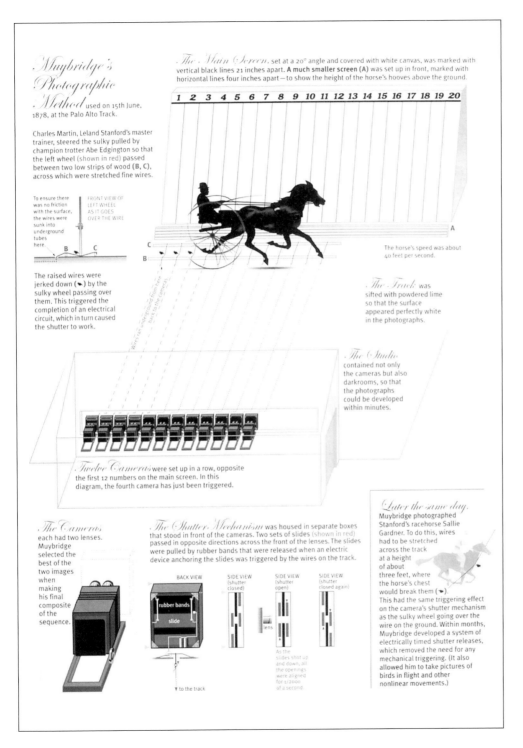

Muybridge's Photographic Method used on 15th June, 1878, at the Palo Alto Track.

Charles Martin, Leland Stanford's master trainer, steered the sulky pulled by champion trotter Abe Edgington so that the left wheel (shown in red) passed between two low strips of wood (B, C), across which were stretched fine wires.

To ensure there was no friction with the surface, the wires were sunk into underground tubes here.

FRONT VIEW OF LEFT WHEEL AS IT GOES OVER THE WIRE

B C

The raised wires were jerked down (↘) by the sulky wheel passing over them. This triggered the completion of an electrical circuit, which in turn caused the shutter to work.

The Main Screen, set at a 20° angle and covered with white canvas, was marked with vertical black lines 21 inches apart. **A much smaller screen (A)** was set up in front, marked with horizontal lines four inches apart—to show the height of the horse's hooves above the ground.

1 2 3 4 5 6 7 8 9 10 11 12 13 14 15 16 17 18 19 20

C
B
A

Wires ran underground from here back to the cameras

The horse's speed was about 40 feet per second.

The Track was sifted with powdered lime so that the surface appeared perfectly white in the photographs.

The Studio contained not only the cameras but also darkrooms, so that the photographs could be developed within minutes.

Twelve Cameras were set up in a row, opposite the first 12 numbers on the main screen. In this diagram, the fourth camera has just been triggered.

The Cameras each had two lenses. Muybridge selected the best of the two images when making his final composite of the sequence.

The Shutter Mechanism was housed in separate boxes that stood in front of the cameras. Two sets of slides (shown in red) passed in opposite directions across the front of the lenses. The slides were pulled by rubber bands that were released when an electric device anchoring the slides was triggered by the wires on the track.

BACK VIEW

rubber bands

slide

↓ to the track

SIDE VIEW (shutter closed)

SIDE VIEW (shutter open)

lens

As the slides shot up and down, all the openings were aligned for 1/2000 of a second.

SIDE VIEW (shutter closed again)

Later the same day, Muybridge photographed Stanford's racehorse Sallie Gardner. To do this, wires had to be stretched across the track at a height of about three feet, where the horse's chest would break them (↘). This had the same triggering effect on the camera's shutter mechanism as the sulky wheel going over the wire on the ground. Within months, Muybridge developed a system of electrically timed shutter releases, which removed the need for any mechanical triggering. (It also allowed him to take pictures of birds in flight and other nonlinear movements.)

A graphic explanation of how Muybridge photographed the horse Abe Edgington pulling a sulky. This was the basic setup he used for the experiments of 1876–79. WRITTEN AND DRAWN BY NIGEL HOLMES/REPRINTED FROM STANFORD MAGAZINE, MAY/JUNE 2001.

motion, the position of the body in equilibrium, which no model could pose for them. . . . My enthusiasm is overflowing.

Producing sequences of subjects in motion marked an important step toward the invention of movies. However, no one had yet found a way to project the pictures one after the other fast enough that the subjects would appear to move. In 1878, Muybridge began making magic lantern slides of his photographs and using them to give illustrated lectures to audiences in California. But these were slide shows of still pictures. To recreate movement, he would need a different kind of apparatus.

In addition to Etienne Marey, several people, among them the editor of *Scientific American* magazine, suggested that Muybridge's sequences of the horse in motion would make beautiful zoetrope strips. In fact, in 1879 the French magazine *L'Illustration* offered to sell bands of Muybridge's horse photographs to be used in a zoetrope. And the American painter Thomas Eakins designed a large, improved zoetrope just to view Muybridge's pictures.

But what Muybridge needed was a projector, and devices like the zoetrope and phenakistiscope were designed for individual viewing, not

projection. Luckily, a small army of inventors had been hard at work on the problem of projection. In addition to Thomas Ross's Wheel of Life, an instrument called the projecting phenakistiscope had been patented in 1869 by the American inventor A. B. Brown, who used it to show sequences of drawings and posed photographs on a phenakistiscope disk. Muybridge made some improvements on these designs and built a projector of his own, which he called the *zoöpraxiscope.* Like other early projectors, it combined a magic lantern with a spinning glass disk. The photographs of the running horse were transferred to this disk, while a second disk served as a slotted shutter that turned in the opposite direction. So as the two disks spun, the awestruck audience watched as the first moving image ever made from instantaneous unposed photographs appeared on the screen—a galloping horse.

Muybridge added other moving subjects to his lectures, including a man juggling and birds flying. His work became well known. In 1881, Muybridge and Stanford published a collection titled *The Attitudes of Animals in Motion.* In the same year, Muybridge traveled to Europe, where he was hailed as a celebrity. In Paris, he was introduced to many influential scientists and inventors. He struck up a close and lasting friendship with Etienne Marey, who would make his own important contributions to the advancement of motion pictures.

Eadweard Muybridge accomplished some remarkable breakthroughs in the photography of moving subjects. However, his methods proved to be a dead end. The technique of using multiple cameras to take a series of photographs of a subject had serious limits, as did using disks for projection. The phenakistiscope and zoöpraxiscope disks could only show endlessly repeated movements of short duration. The technology would have to progress a little further before true movies could be made, but by the 1860s and 1870s, more and more people were beginning to envision where all these advances were taking them. ✳

Muybridge's Great Motion Studies

Following his early success, Muybridge continued and expanded his work. He took a position at the University of Pennsylvania in 1884 and began work on a project that would become, three years later, a massive study of animals in motion—including the human type. It bore the formidable title *Animal Locomotion: An Electro-Photographic Investigation of Consecutive Phases of Animal Movements, 1872–1885.* Human subjects were photographed performing all kinds of actions, such as walking, running, climbing stairs, wrestling, dancing, and fencing. In many cases, the subjects were nude so that the movements of the limbs and the attitude of the body could be clearly seen.

··❧ 7 ❦··
Etienne-Jules Marey
and the First True Films

While Eadweard Muybridge was busy in America lining up his batteries of cameras and photographing everything that moved, a different, but equally important, kind of discovery was being made across the Atlantic. In France, Etienne-Jules Marey (1830–1904) was also working on the problem of how to record the movements of living things.

GRAPHING MOTION

Marey was neither a photographer nor a showman. He wasn't aiming to make movies. He was a physiologist: a scientist interested in studying how organisms function. Marey was searching for a more accurate way than direct observation to study the movements of living things. He wanted to be able to record and measure everything from the beat of the heart to the action of a bird in flight. The human senses, he thought, were insufficient for precise observation and measurement. "How can one feel the delicate nuances of the pulse with the finger?" he wrote. In a book titled *La méthode graphique dans les sciences expérimentales et principalement en physiologie et en médecine* (The graphic method in the

Marey's chronophotographic camera. COLLÈGE DE FRANCE

97

experimental sciences and principally in physiology and medicine), published in 1878, Marey explained his thinking further:

Not only are these instruments sometimes destined to replace the observer . . . but they also have their own domain where nothing can replace them. When the eye ceases to see, the ear to hear, touch to feel, or indeed when our senses give deceptive appearances, these instruments are like new senses of astonishing precision.

Marey thought that the photographic technology available at the time was too slow for his purposes, so he turned to other means of recording motion. He constructed instruments similar to the modern polygraph, or lie detector, that would inscribe the movements of his subjects as squiggly lines on a graph. Changes in a subject's position would be transmitted to a needle that would trace a chart of the movement on paper. Marey called this technique *chronography,* a word derived from the Greek *chronos,* meaning "time," and *grapho,* "I write."

Marey attempted many ambitious projects, devising various instruments for different purposes. To study the human walk, for example, he built a shoe with an air-filled chamber in the sole. When the foot hit the ground, the air was forced through a tube, which caused the needle on the recording instrument to twitch, creating a graph. In this way, Marey could analyze the graphs and study such things as how body weight affected the way a person walked. This arrangement was a little awkward because the subject had to carry a bulky load of equipment. But it did work.

Marey applied his methods to all sorts of creatures. Using various versions of his chronographs, he was able to show, as Muybridge had, that all four feet of a galloping horse do indeed leave the ground. With very delicate instruments, he even measured the movements of insects' wings.

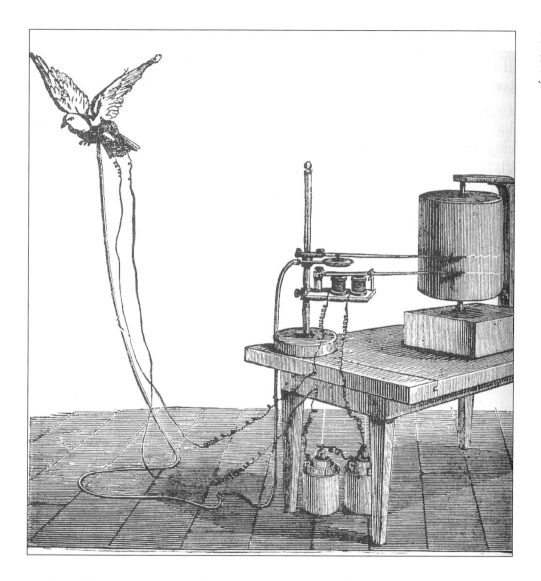

But Marey's most amazing feat was to record the movements of birds in flight. To do this, he made a sort of vest for the bird, which registered the expansion and contraction of the breast muscles. What's more, on each wing there was a tiny device that opened and closed an electrical circuit in response to the flapping of the wings. Thus outfitted, the bird was allowed to fly, and the movement of its muscles and wings set the recording instrument in motion.

Marey achieved great advances in the analysis of movement, but he dreamed of having actual photographs that would reflect what he had recorded in his graphs. Although there had been some recent improvements in cameras and light-sensitive emulsions, he still believed that photography was incapable of the instantaneous exposures needed to freeze rapid motion. So to recreate lifelike images, he asked a friend to make a series of meticulous drawings of a running horse based on his graphs. He then put these drawings in a zoetrope to reproduce the action. "These pictures placed in the instrument give a complete illusion and show a horse which strolls, walks or trots as the case may be," he remarked.

For a while, these drawings satisfied Marey's desire for a lifelike image. But he couldn't resist the allure of photography for long.

In 1873, the French press reported Muybridge's success in photographing Stanford's horse Occident. At about the same time, a friend of Marey's named Alphonse Penaud suggested a way to use photography to study the flight of birds. Penaud was interested in flight for his own reasons: he was a pioneer of aviation. In fact, in 1876 he patented a design for a helicopter. But in this case, his interests and Marey's overlapped.

Inspiration from yet another source may have triggered Penaud's idea. In 1873, astronomers were busily preparing for a rare occurrence—the passage of the planet Venus across the face of the sun, which would happen on December 9, 1874. There was a great deal of excitement in the scientific community because as the planet passed across the sun, astronomers would be able to calculate the true distance of the sun from the earth. All kinds of scientific instruments were assembled to record and measure the event. Among them was a strange device invented by a French astronomer with the imposing name Pierre-Jules-César Janssen.

Janssen called the device a *photographic revolver*. As the name suggests, it was a camera shaped roughly like a revolver. Images were recorded on a disk similar to those Plateau had used in his phenakisti-scope. When the operator "pulled the trigger" a clockwork mechanism drove the disk around in a stop-start motion. The stop-start movement of the disk was synchronized with a shutter, so that each time the disk stopped, the shutter would open and a photograph would be taken. This remarkable contraption could take forty-eight photographs in only seventy-two seconds.

On December 9, Janssen succeeded in capturing the passage of Venus across the sun with his revolver. Marey was intrigued by this, but still had doubts that the exposure time of the photographic revolver was fast enough to capture the flight of birds.

THE REVOLVER BECOMES A RIFLE

A few years later, when Muybridge's 1878 photographs of a horse in motion appeared in *La Nature,* Marey began to change his mind. He was impressed. In his letter to the editor of the journal, Marey asked to be put in touch with Muybridge. He wrote, "I was dreaming of a kind of *photographic gun,* to seize the bird in a pose or, even better, in a series of poses marking the successive phases of the movement of its wings. . . . It is clearly an easy experiment for Mr. Muybridge."

When Muybridge met Marey in Paris in 1881, Muybridge presented him with a series of photographs of a bird in flight. Marey was delighted, but he was dissatisfied with the clarity of the images, which were inferior to Muybridge's photographs of horses. Marey concluded that "it is not possible to apply to the free flight of a bird the same method used for the horse, which consists of the animal itself breaking electric wires spaced along its path."

In other words, birds didn't adapt as well as horses to a controlled environment. They couldn't be made to run along a track laid with trip wires and batteries of cameras.

A portrait of Etienne-Jules Marey taken in 1878. COLLÈGE DE FRANCE

Marey was convinced to pursue photography anyway, in spite of its limitations. However, he chose a different approach from Muybridge. He decided to go ahead and construct a photographic rifle based on Janssen's design. If successful, it would allow him to take a rapid series of pictures on a disk by aiming his camera at the bird as he would a rifle. The result was an instrument capable of taking twelve images per second at the relatively fast exposure of $1/720$ of a second.

Although it was still restricted by the number of pictures that could fit on a disk, the rifle was a big jump forward from Muybridge's cumbersome batteries of cameras. It was light, portable, and easy to use. With it, Marey photographed birds, animals, and people, creating series of pictures that could reproduce natural motion. These studies had great practical value. For instance, being able to observe the changes in birds' wings under different conditions led to a greater understanding of aerodynamics.

A man practicing with a photographic rifle. It really did look like a rifle, and could be aimed like one, with the butt held against the shoulder. There was a lens in the barrel, and a viewfinder for sighting. COLLÈGE DE FRANCE

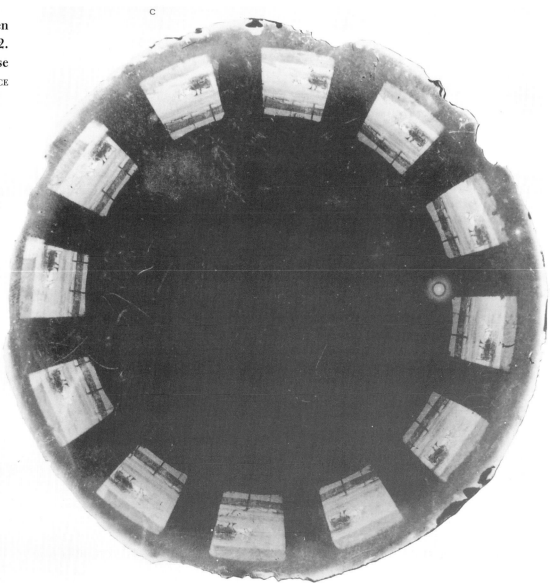

A circular disk of photographs taken with a photographic rifle in 1882. The barely visible image is of a horse pulling a carriage. COLLÈGE DE FRANCE

Even though Marey succeeded in getting useful images, he was still not entirely happy with the quality of the results. The photographs were little more than silhouettes and lacked the detail he desired. But rather than give up on photography, he simply began exploring ways to make better cameras and get higher quality photographs.

MOVEMENT IN A SINGLE FRAME

In 1882, Marey established an institution called the Station Physiologique—a center for the study of physiology, particularly of the body in motion. He was assisted by a man named Georges Demeny, a leading advocate of physical education in France. By this time, Marey's commitment to photography was strong enough that his institution included a large photography studio, thirty-six feet long and thirteen feet high, open at one end. The walls were hung with black velvet.

The Station Physiologique was amply funded by the Paris City Council, which had its own reasons for putting up the money. As one council member put it, "One may study scientifically . . . the question of the best footwear to give our soldiers."

Marey now had all the space and equipment he needed. In his new workshop and laboratory, he designed another kind of camera—one that could take a series of pictures very rapidly on a *single* photographic plate. This camera was capable of exposures of $\frac{1}{1000}$ of a second. To improve the detail in the photographs, he dressed his subjects in white and photographed them against the black background. At other times, he dressed them in black with strips of shiny metal along the outlines of the body, so that only the strips would be recorded by the camera. Marey's results were similar to modern photographs made with a stroboscopic light that show, in one picture, multiple images of, say, a golf swing or a pole vaulter's leap. These pictures afforded yet another means of studying moving subjects.

The photographs Marey took in this way had several advantages over anything done before. They were clearer and more detailed than either Muybridge's or those Marey had taken earlier with the photographic rifle. And unlike Muybridge with his batteries of cameras, Marey was able to photograph his subjects from a single point of view, using just one camera. Finally, Marey's camera made exposures at regular intervals

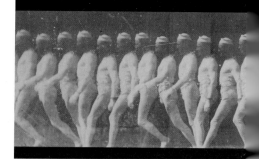

THE MASTER AND HIS ASSISTANT

This multiple exposure shows Marey's assistant Georges Demeny, with whom he had a bitter falling out. It was one of those squabbles between the master and his assistant that arise when the assistant decides to strike out on his own. Demeny needed cameras patented by Marey for his own research, but according to Demeny, Marey balked at setting up a partnership that would allow it. So Demeny made a technical change in Marey's camera and filed for his own patent. Demeny had come up with a better mechanism for driving the film through the projector. However, Marey accused Demeny of stealing his design and demanded his resignation. Demeny refused but was eventually fired. It was a sordid end to a working collaboration that had contributed so much to the advancement of motion pictures.

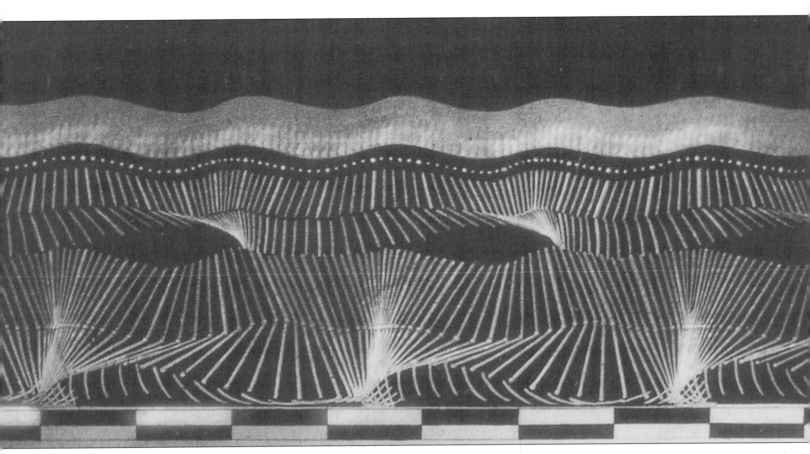

In this multiple exposure on a single plate of a soldier walking, only the white stripes painted on the man's clothing reflect the light and thus register on the film.
COLLÈGE DE FRANCE

that were determined by the operator, not by the pace of a horse tripping wires laid across a track.

FINALLY . . . FILM!

In 1884, a product was invented that had as much impact on photography in the nineteenth century as digital photography has had in the twenty-first. The product was film. Up to this time, each photograph required an individual plate—the earliest plates were metal, but were soon supplanted by glass plates. From the 1850s to the late 1870s, most photography was done with glass, using the wet-plate process. There were many efforts to make dry plates, but they were unsuccessful because the light-sensitive material that was in use lost its sensitivity as it dried. Experimenters worked for years to solve this problem, and finally did in the late 1870s. Around 1880, dry plates went on the market. Now everything no longer had to be done in the field. A photographer could leave the burro and the wagon behind, grab a stack of dry plates, go and take pictures, then process the plates in the comfort of home.

In 1885, a dry-plate manufacturer in Rochester, New York, named George Eastman pushed the dry process a step further. He came out with strips of "film," which were made of paper coated with a light-sensitive gelatin emulsion. It was called *American film*.

Marey saw immediately that Eastman's paper film would lend itself perfectly to his work, and he set about designing a new camera that could use it. On October 15, 1888, he announced to the French Academy of Sciences, "I hope to obtain a series of images on a long strip of sensitized paper, moved with a rapid translatory motion and stopped at the moments of exposure." Two weeks later, he showed his first film at the Academy—a strip of paper with a series of photographs on it.

As revolutionary as it was, the American film was awkward to use because the paper backing had to be stripped off after the film was processed. But that problem didn't last long. Just two years after introducing the product, Eastman produced a transparent film composed of a gelatin emulsion on a celluloid base—in appearance, much like modern film. It had been invented by a pastor named Hannibal Goodwin, who wanted a better material for showing magic lantern slides to his Sunday school classes. Eastman bought the rights from Goodwin and began commercial production.

GEORGE EASTMAN'S KODAK

The inventor of American film was the same George Eastman who would become famous in 1888 with the introduction of a small hand camera that anyone could use. It was called the *Kodak*. Eastman's Kodak finally brought photography to the masses. By this time emulsions had been made sensitive enough that anyone could take instantaneous pictures of people and animals in daylight with a simple camera. "You push the button and we do the rest," proclaimed the Kodak motto: Take a roll of pictures, send camera and film to the lab, get back finished pictures and a camera reloaded with enough film for a hundred exposures.

Marey obtained a supply of this film in 1890, constructed an improved camera, and went to work taking photographs in earnest. One advantage of this new method was that it was portable—Marey could take his camera anywhere. He explained:

Using this method, one may operate in front of all types of background, illuminated or dark; this allows the study of movements which it is of interest to know in the place where they occur. In this way one will capture the movements of practitioners of different trades in the factory, those of runners and gymnasts on their training grounds, those of all kinds of animals in menageries and zoological gardens.

THE FINAL STEP: PROJECTION

Marey had succeeded in making what could be considered the first movies—photographs taken in rapid sequence on a strip of film. However, to view these movies he had to cut out each picture and glue it to a zoetrope drum. No projector existed that would handle strips of film; there were only projectors, like Muybridge's zoöpraxiscope, that used disks. The zoetrope was sufficient for studying the films, but like Muybridge and others, Marey wanted to be able to show them to large audiences. So once again, the inventor set to work.

A projector is just the reverse of a camera. The film passes behind the lens, just as it does in a camera. But in a projector, the light shines from behind the film out through the lens. Since a movie is a rapid sequence of still pictures, each frame must be projected as a still picture. That means that each frame on the film has to stop briefly—for a tiny fraction of a second—when it reaches the point directly behind the lens, and at the same time the shutter has to open to allow the light to shine through the lens. So the projector needs a drive mechanism that will stop and start the film at the right place at the right speed. This problem plagued Marey. He wrote to Georges Demeny, his assistant, on January 21, 1892, "My projection apparatus is proceeding gradually through some appalling difficulties."

Marey finally did produce a machine that worked. He called it the *chronophotographic projector;* it was actually a reversible camera, which could be used to both take and project pictures. But he was not altogether pleased with the results. A big part of the problem lay with the film itself. The images on the film were not evenly spaced, so when it was run through the projector, figures appeared to jump around a little bit. The problem was complicated by the lack of a precise drive mechanism.

For Marey, moving pictures were a scientific tool, a way of seeing what our eyes cannot see. But even though he wasn't interested in movies as such, his inventions helped to establish film as a medium of entertainment and education. The chronophotographic projector was the last of Marey's many technical contributions to the birth of motion pictures. But during the early 1890s, there were plenty of others busily at work trying to solve the mechanical problems that had so frustrated him. ✳

❧ 8 ☙

The Rush to the Movies

During the 1880s, news of Muybridge's and Marey's successes set off a flurry of activity. Inventors on both sides of the Atlantic, many of them now long forgotten, labored feverishly to make better cameras and projectors. It was becoming clear to more and more people that moving pictures were within reach, if only they could solve a few technical problems. These were the same problems that had bedeviled Marey: How to take a rapid series of pictures on film and at the same time give each frame enough exposure to produce a clear image, and how to design a mechanism that would move the film along with the regular, stop-and-go motion that was needed.

TECHNICAL DIFFICULTIES

Dozens of clever solutions were tried, most of them eventually abandoned. There were cameras that used a pressure pad that would slap against the film as it ran through the machine, stopping it briefly in its passage. There were others that drove the film with a version of an eccentric cam—a disk mounted off center on a rotating shaft that moved the film with a jerky, stop-start motion. But none of these machines was

A poster for Emile Reynaud's *Pantomimes Lumineuses,* the first animated movies. LIBRARY OF CONGRESS, PRINTS AND PHOTOGRAPHS DIVISION able to move the film with enough accuracy to give a perfectly clear image.

Meanwhile, some inventors tried to sidestep the problem by eliminating moving film altogether. They did this by building cameras with multiple lenses. The question of how to drive the film was avoided by having the strip of film remain stationary behind a row of lenses. By rapidly exposing the film through one lens after another, a series of pictures would be taken. This solution amounted to condensing Muybridge's series of cameras into one camera with multiple lenses. But it turned out to be just as impractical.

Around 1883, a Frenchman named Albert Londe designed a camera that had nine lenses mounted in a ring. A few years later, in 1886, Louis Aimé Augustin Le Prince (1842–1890?) filed for an American patent on a camera with sixteen lenses arranged in two panels of eight. Behind each panel was a strip of film on rollers. The film didn't move during exposure. Instead, the eight electromagnetic shutters behind the eight lenses in each panel were fired one after the other. It took one second to fire all eight. Then the second set of shutters would fire, and while this was happening a mechanism would shift a new strip of film into place behind the first one.

INVENTORS AT THE DOOR

Le Prince had been told that a camera had to expose the film at sixteen frames per second to give an impression of smooth motion when projected, so he built his camera to do just that. His 1886 application for a U.S. patent was finally granted in 1888, but he soon abandoned the idea and turned his efforts to building a single-lens camera. We can only assume that the complex mechanism turned out to be too cumbersome. No film taken with the sixteen-lens camera has ever been found.

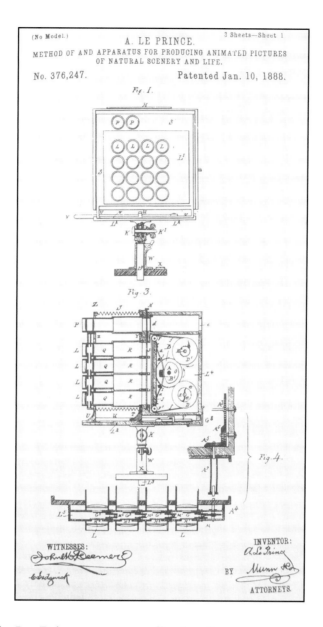

Le Prince's patent for his sixteen-lens camera. UNITED STATES PATENT AND TRADEMARK OFFICE

It is possible that Louis Le Prince was actually the first person to make and project a photographic film—in 1888, two years before Marey. He made some films using Eastman's paper strips and a single-lens camera of his own design, and the date October 1888 is handwritten on the paper backing. If the date is correct, one of his films, which lasts about

A drawing from Wordsworth Donisthorpe's 1891 U.S. patent for the Kinesigraph. This is a side view, showing the barrel of the lens and the various pulleys and belts and cranks needed to move the film. United States Patent and Trademark Office

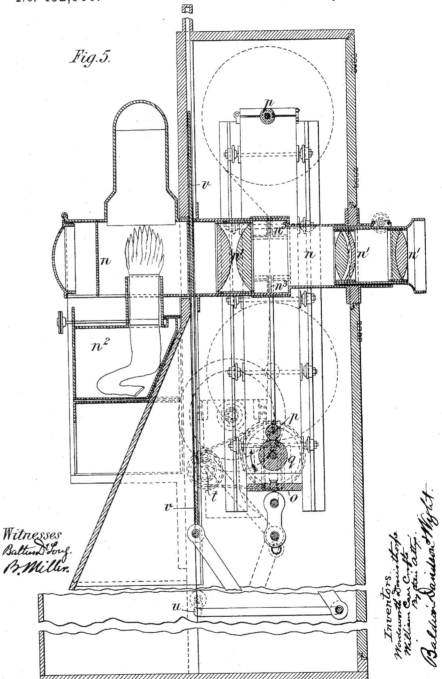

W. DONISTHORPE & W. C. CROFTS.

METHOD OF PRODUCING INSTANTANEOUS PHOTOGRAPHS.

No. 452,966.　　　　　　　　　　　Patented May 26, 1891.

Fig.5.

three seconds, is the earliest piece of film in existence. It is a street scene of a busy road in the city of Leeds, England. The scene is full of activity—people walking, carriages and wagons bearing passengers and freight.

There are also Le Prince films from around the same time of a group of people in a garden belonging to his father-in-law, Joseph Whitley, and of a man playing a concertina. Le Prince showed his films privately to the workers in his father-in-law's factory, where he had his workshop, but he never presented them to the public.

These films were of a different order than Marey's careful scientific studies. They were casual pictures of everyday life, closer to the films shown by the Lumière brothers in 1895, and they foreshadowed a new direction in visual entertainment.

Another promising camera was designed by an English barrister (lawyer) named Wordsworth Donisthorpe (1847/8–1914). He filed a patent in 1876 for a camera that drove the film at a constant stop-start rate, so that the distance between frames was perfectly equal. It seems that the inspiration for Donisthorpe's camera came from the textile industry. His father was an inventor of wool-combing machines, and apparently Donisthorpe adapted the mechanism from these machines to photography. Donisthorpe called his camera the *Kinesigraph*. In 1890, he made a film of Trafalgar Square in London that was quite successful, but it was never projected. Only ten frames of this film have survived.

Unfortunately, Donisthorpe was unable to obtain financial backing to continue his experiments. Sir George Newnes, to whom he applied for funding, was told by the "experts" he consulted that the idea was "wild, visionary and ridiculous," and that the only result of attempting to photograph motion would be "an undescribable blur."

There were many other early experimenters, but one in particular deserves mention. He was a German magic lantern artist named Max

Skladanowsky (1863–1939). He and his father and his brother Emil formed a company called Nebula Pictures. They specialized in lantern shows of natural disasters: earthquakes, fires, thunderstorms, and so on.

Max Skladanowsky invented a movie camera he called the *Bioscope.* Using George Eastman's celluloid film, in 1892 he filmed his brother Emil dancing on the roof of the family house in Berlin. The Bioscope was a two-lens camera. It could take only eight frames per second, so two lenses and two strips of film were needed to reach the necessary sixteen. After the film was shot, each strip had to be cut into individual frames, then reassembled, first a frame from one strip, then a frame from the other, and so forth. This was a tedious procedure that wasn't likely to take the art of film much further than the ten-second strips that Skladanowsky pasted together.

Like other cameras that used more than one lens, Skladanowsky's Bioscope didn't have much of a future, but one important event insured that this man would not be forgotten. Even though history has honored the Lumière brothers as the first to give a public showing of movies, Skladanowsky actually showed his films almost two months earlier. He gave a public performance at the Wintergarten in Berlin on November 1, 1895. The show featured nine films, ten seconds each, of such subjects as a children's folk dance, a juggler, gymnasts, and a boxing kangaroo.

For a couple of years Skladanowsky toured Europe with his Bioscope show, but his invention was soon outdated, overtaken by the single-lens cameras of the Lumières and others.

THE OPTICAL THEATER OF EMILE REYNAUD

While these inventors, and many others, were struggling with their cameras and projectors to bring film and photography together, Emile Reynaud, the inventor of the praxinoscope, was working his own way into film history. Well before the Lumières' Paris debut, Reynaud was giving public performances of fifteen-minute films, in color, that told a complete story. Why isn't he considered "the father of motion pictures"? For one reason only: His films were hand drawn.

By 1880, Reynaud had developed a working projection praxinoscope. When he presented this machine to the French Photographic Society, he also suggested that the society work on the problem of projecting animated photographs in place of hand-drawn images. However, in his own work, Reynaud seemed more interested in his colorful hand-painted strips than in photographs like Muybridge's, which were black and white and lacking in detail. So he devoted his time to developing the praxinoscope into a powerful projector that could show hand-painted films of greater length.

Up to this time, all the various devices for animating pictures, like the zoetrope, could only show short actions that repeated themselves over and over. For example, Muybridge's horses ran in place, repeating exactly the same movements. But in 1888, Reynaud made a revolutionary breakthrough. In the same year that Louis Le Prince made his first movies on paper film and Etienne Marey unveiled his chronophotographic projector, Reynaud invented a machine he called the *Théâtre Optique*. It was a large praxinoscope capable of projecting long strips. His French patent describes its purpose:

> *The aim of the device is to obtain the illusion of movement, no longer limited to the repetition of the same positions at each rotation of the instrument, as necessarily produced by all known apparatus (zoetropes, praxinoscopes, etc.), but having on the contrary an indefinite variety and duration and in this way producing true animated scenes of unlimited development.*

An engraving of Emile Reynaud projecting a film with his Théâtre
Optique. LIBRARY OF CONGRESS, PRINTS AND PHOTOGRAPHS DIVISION

Reynaud was talking about making movies—real movies, not just endlessly repeated actions. How was he able to do this in 1888? He did it by painting his pictures individually on transparent gelatin squares, and then attaching them to leather bands, making a continuous strip. The strip was then wound on rollers.

Not only did Reynaud create the first continuous animated film, but he also devised a way of driving the strip through the projector, which solved the problems that had frustrated so many others. He perforated his strips. With holes along the edge at regular intervals, the strips were moved with precision through the projector by a wheel with pins, something like the sprocket on a bicycle, that engaged the perforations.

Reynaud was ahead of his time. It wasn't until three years later, in 1891, that George Eastman marketed the first commercially made perforated film, making possible a more accurate movement of the film through the camera and projector.

Reynaud tried to sell his equipment to the managers of theaters and fairgrounds but had little success. Finally, he decided to put on public shows himself, and in 1892 he signed a contract to use a hall in the Musée Grévin, a famous wax museum in Paris. He called his shows *Pantomimes Lumineuses.*

These were elaborate productions that combined his animated films with many of the techniques developed by magic lanternists. All projection was done from behind the screen, so none of the apparatus was visible to the audience. The Théâtre Optique was used to project the moving images, while the fixed background was provided by a magic lantern. There were sound effects, which were synchronized with the film by means of silver strips along the film's edge. These strips activated an electromagnet, which in turn triggered a noise gen-

The Sad End of Emile Reynaud

Emile Reynaud (*above*) has been described as a filmmaker whose work was unsurpassed until Walt Disney started making animated movies in the 1930s. However, when filmed movies became all the rage, Reynaud's popularity fell off, and in 1900 the Musée Grévin canceled his shows. Reynaud then entered a long period of depression. In 1912 he sold all of his equipment, some of it for scrap. He kept one Théâtre Optique, but a year later he smashed it to pieces with a hammer and threw all but two of his films into the Seine. He died penniless in a house for the poor on January 9, 1918.

erator. Special live music was also composed and performed for these productions.

Reynaud's films lasted from twelve to fifteen minutes, and it was painstaking work to make them. A twelve-minute film required seven hundred different poses painted on seven hundred individual gelatin squares. Today's animated movies and TV shows, like *The Simpsons* and *South Park,* are made in the same way—by drawing a series of pictures, each one slightly different from the one before it. The basic principle hasn't changed. But Reynaud did all the work himself. Modern full-length animated movies, or even a half-hour TV show, are made by teams of animators who follow a highly organized, well-established procedure. Each step of the animation process, from the first sketchy storyboard to the finished film, has been developed from years of experience, beginning early in the twentieth century. Now, once a series of pictures is finished, each drawing is photographed with a single-frame movie camera to make the film. More recently, digital imaging has even made it possible for computers to create animated images from just a group of photographs. A subject is photographed from many angles and in many different poses, all of which are fed into a computer. Using this information, the computer program can then put the subject in motion.

Reynaud's films were humorous or satirical sketches, as most animated films and cartoons have been since then. They dealt with such themes as romantic intrigues and the antics of clowns. One of his earliest films was called *Un Bon Bok* (A Good Beer). It is set in a Paris bistro, where a gentleman is trying to romance the pretty waitress. She resists, he pursues, and the game goes on. Taking advantage of this diversion, a kitchen boy sneaks in and drinks the man's beer.

Although the realism of the photograph would eventually become more popular, Reynaud's films were the first real movies. They told complete stories and were full of color and sound and movement.

They were far more lively than the first photographic films. Reynaud was also technically ahead of his time. While others struggled with all sorts of odd contraptions for taking and projecting pictures, Reynaud was happily showing his handmade movies to delighted crowds. ✳

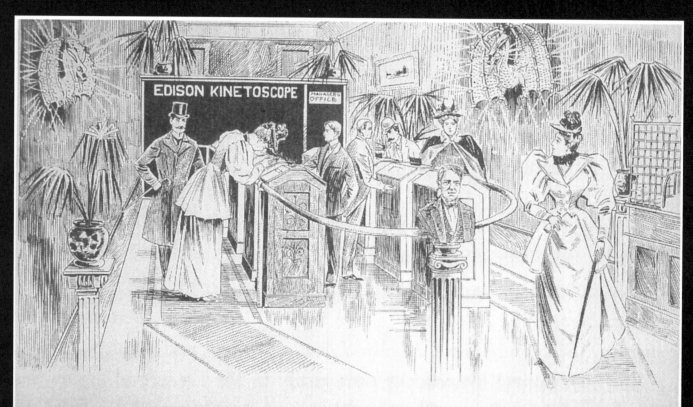

Interior of Kinetoscope parlor at 1155 Broadway, near 28th Street, New York, operated by the Kinetoscope Co., controlling the United States and Canada. The first Kinetoscope exhibition started in the world; opened April 14, 1894.

··❧ ❂ ❧··
Thomas Edison and
the American Movie Machine

The year 1895 was a busy one in the history of movies. The Lumières grabbed the headlines with their show at the Grand Café, but there were plenty of others churning out new ideas for cameras and projectors. Inventors in England, Germany, and the United States had all produced working machines at roughly the same time. In this atmosphere, it's no surprise that inventors working on the same problems borrowed—and sometimes outright stole—from one another. No one worked in isolation, and no one could legitimately claim to be the sole inventor of anything.

Although the Lumières' debut focused attention on Europe, American inventors had been busy in their workshops for some time. At this point, projection was the goal of practically everyone working on making films—with one notable exception. America's most acclaimed inventor, the man often hailed as the father of American movies, was strangely absent from the race. His name was Thomas Alva Edison (1847–1931).

A drawing of a Kinetoscope parlor, clearly intended to appeal to a respectable clientele. A bust of Edison himself stands guard in the foreground.
LIBRARY OF CONGRESS, PRINTS AND PHOTOGRAPHS DIVISION

A portrait of young Thomas Edison with his phonograph, taken around 1878.

Edison had been interested in moving pictures since the late 1880s. His first efforts were directed toward combining pictures and sound based on the design of the phonograph, which he had invented in 1877. In 1888, Eadweard Muybridge visited Edison at his laboratories in West Orange, New Jersey, to propose a collaboration to combine his zoöpraxiscope with Edison's phonograph. Edison declined the offer, probably because he saw that Muybridge's machine was too limited, but shortly thereafter he instructed his talented young assistant, William Kennedy Laurie Dickson, to work on the problem of combining film with recorded sound. He also filed a caveat (a formal notice) with the Patents Office on October 17, 1888, outlining his plans for a machine that, in his words, would "do for the eye what the phonograph does for the ear." He called it the *Kinetoscope.*

Dickson began the project by modeling his apparatus on the phonograph, using a rotating cylinder (this was before phonograph disks) both to photograph and to view the pictures. To accomplish this, the photographs had to be tiny—about one-sixteenth of an inch across—which meant that they had to be taken and viewed through a microscope lens. The pictures would be arranged in a spiral on the cylinder, following the pattern of the grooves that recorded the sound. Dickson struggled with this device through most of 1889, and a few of these early Kinetoscopes were produced. But the quality of sound was poor and the image was blurred and shaky.

In August 1889, Edison left for France. Already famous for his inventions of the phonograph and the electric light, he had been invited to attend the Exposition Universelle, an exhibition of all the latest advances in technology and science. In France, Edison met Etienne-Jules Marey, who served as his guide to the exposition and gave him a tour of the exhibition of French photography. Three hundred participants were displaying their photographs and equipment. Marey also showed Edison his pictures of people and animals in motion, as well as those of the flight of birds. And he demonstrated his chronographic strips and cameras. It is likely that Edison also saw Reynaud's Théâtre Optique, which used strips of film perforated along the edges.

THE EDISON KINETOSCOPE

Edison was obviously impressed, for on his return to West Orange he immediately wrote a new caveat for the Patent Office describing a

THE KINETOSCOPE

The *Kinetoscope* functioned both as camera and viewer. It was a large wooden cabinet, weighing about 150 pounds, with a hole on top through which the viewer looked. Below the peep hole was a lens that magnified the image. An electric motor drove at a constant speed under the lens, and a rapidly rotating shutter with a small window cut into it flashed to the viewer the image on each frame as it passed by. Each image lasted just a split second. Underneath the film was an electric light in a reflector, which illuminated the image.

In his patent of 1891, Edison specified the width of the film strips as 35 millimeters—the same width used to this day in high-quality commercial films and the most popular still cameras.

Thomas Edison's sketch for a projector using perforated film. This was part of the caveat submitted to the Patent Office shortly after he visited Paris in 1889.

EDISON NATIONAL HISTORIC SITE

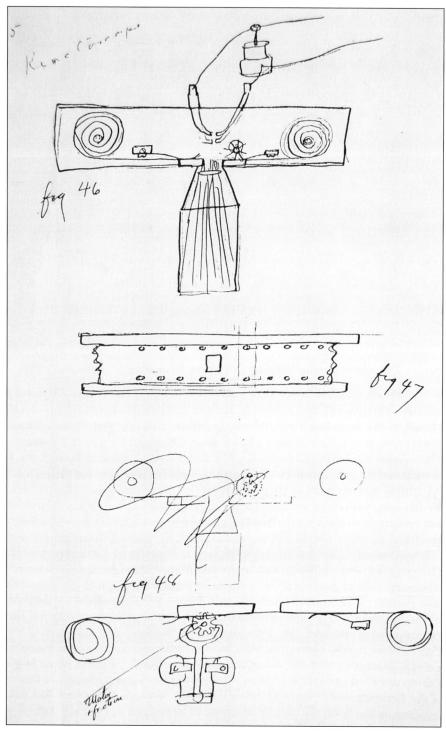

machine that would use strips of transparent film, perforated on both edges. The film would be driven past the lens by a toothed sprocket that would engage the perforations in the film. Dickson was set to work on constructing such a camera, but progress was slow because he was still tinkering with the earlier model. Finally, on May 20, 1891, the new machine was ready, and a group from the National Federation of Women's Clubs, who were visiting Edison's laboratories, was treated to the first demonstration.

They saw, through an aperture in a pine box standing on the floor, the picture of a man. It bowed and smiled, and took off its hat naturally and gracefully. Every motion was perfect, without a hitch or a jerk.

The bowing, smiling man was none other than William Dickson himself.

Edison wasted no time taking his Kinetoscope into mass production. It was basically a peep show with movies—a large box with a viewing hole in the top through which, for a nickel, a person could watch a short film. It was marketed as a slot machine—the "Nickel-in-the-Slot Kinetoscope," Dickson dubbed it—and in April 1894, the Holland brothers in New York City bought ten machines and set up the first video arcade. For fifty cents the customer could see ten different films with such titles as *Trapeze, The Barbershop, Sandow* (a famous strongman), and *Horse Shoeing*. Within the next two months Kinetoscope parlors opened in Chicago and San Francisco, and by the end of the year most major American cities sported at least one. Kinetoscopes also appeared in hotels, restaurants, and bars. They were a huge success. Edison was doing so well with this machine that he considered it much more profitable than projected movies could ever be. But he was wrong, and he soon changed his course.

Edison's Black Maria was the first studio designed for making commercial films.
Since photographic film was still relatively slow, the roof was designed so that it
could open to let in light, and the building was set on a revolving platform so
that the stage where filming took place could stay aligned with the sun.
EDISON NATIONAL HISTORIC SITE

EDISON'S FILM FACTORY

The soaring demand for Kinetoscopes led naturally to a soaring demand
for more films. To meet this demand Edison built a studio in West Orange,
an ugly, tar-coated, windowless shed that was named the Black Maria,
which at that time was slang for paddy wagon, the black wagons used by
the police.

William Dickson, along with a collaborator named William Heise,
made most of the films at the Black Maria. The majority of them were
simply filmed versions of acts from the vaudeville variety shows: a
strongman, a couple of contortionists, an animal trainer, Annabelle
Whitford's Butterfly Dance, and Annie Oakley and Native American

dancers from Buffalo Bill's Wild West Show. But Dickson and Heise also made films of everyday life, like a barbershop scene and a dentist pulling a tooth. Violent sporting events were produced for men: boxing matches, knife fights, cockfights, and barroom brawls. And in addition to violence, of course, there were "naughty" films, which treated the viewer to bare ankles and belly dancers.

CHALLENGES TO EDISON

The success of Edison's Kinetoscope soon attracted competitors. In 1894, a New York businessman named Otway Latham founded the Kinetoscope Exhibition Company and established his own viewing parlor. He soon drew his brother Gray; his father, Major Woodville Latham; and his old friend Enoch Rector into the company. Using machines ordered from Edison, they specialized in filming boxing matches, which became very popular and were shown in cities across the United States. It immediately occurred to the Lathams that they could do better by projecting their films with a magic lantern for a paying audience. To make their projector, they enlisted the best technician around for the job—Edison's assistant William Dickson. Edison still thought there was no future in projection, but Dickson disagreed and took the opportunity to work for the Lathams. As a result, he found himself in the awkward position of working for a competitor while still on Edison's payroll. When Edison learned of this, his temper flared, and like Marey and Demeny before them, the two parted bitterly the following year.

In the Lathams' workshop, the collaborators, led by Dickson and Rector, designed and built an improved camera, different enough from Edison's Kinetoscope to avoid a patent dispute, and a projector they christened the Eidoloscope. The Latham brothers used the Eidoloscope to give the first American showing of a film by projection in April 1895, eight months before the Lumières' debut in Paris. It was a short clip of

These frames from an 1894 Edison
Kinetoscope film feature the dancer
Annabelle Whitford.

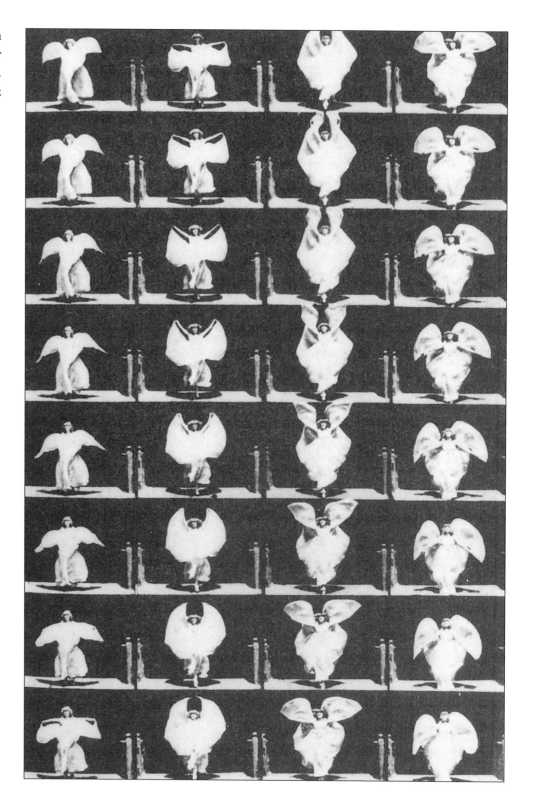

boys playing in a park. In May, the brothers opened a small storefront theater and exhibited for a paying audience a boxing match filmed on the roof of Madison Square Garden. The Lathams' films were of poor quality—small and dim—but they were enough of a challenge that an angry Thomas Edison cried fraud, accused the Lathams of stealing his ideas, and threatened them with a lawsuit. He promised that in a few months he would have much better films, life-size and with sound. In spite of Edison's threats, the Lathams kept showing their films and even went into mass production.

The Lathams weren't the only competitors in America who were working on projecting films. Two unlikely candidates, a real estate agent named Thomas Armat and a stenographer named Charles Francis Jenkins, formed a partnership, and in August 1895 they submitted a patent application for a machine they called a *Phantoscope* (no relation to Robert's magic lantern Fantascope). Armat and Jenkins gave public exhibitions with the Phantoscope in Atlanta, Georgia, using Edison's films.

PROJECTION WINS OUT

The Phantoscope show was probably of low quality, since it used films designed for the Kinetoscope rather than for projection. In the Kinetoscope, the light is directly behind the film, which gives bright illumination to the image. But when film is projected, the image grows dimmer the farther the projector is from the screen. Nevertheless, the Phantoscope was praised in the press, and its success seems to have convinced Edison that the future lay with projection, not peep shows. Taking the short route, Edison bought the patent rights to the Phantoscope from Armat and Jenkins and changed its name to the *Vitascope*. What's more, one of the conditions of the sale was that Edison would receive sole credit for its invention. So Armat and Jenkins quietly disappeared, the Phantoscope became the Vitascope—which was hailed in the press as

A poster advertising Thomas Edison's Vitascope promises "Pictures life size and full of color." Since no color process existed at the time, some filmmakers had their films colored by hand with transparent watercolors.

LIBRARY OF CONGRESS, PRINTS AND PHOTOGRAPHS DIVISION

Edison's new wonder—and the Wizard of West Orange was in the movie business.

Soon a bewildering conglomeration of "-scopes" and "-graphs" crowded into the field, and music halls and hastily converted storefronts filled to bursting with eager spectators. Other devices in use around this time included an updated version of the Lathams' Eidoloscope, the Lumières' Cinématographe, and something called the *Kineopticon,* invented by an American named Birt Acres.

Meanwhile, Edison's former assistant William Dickson had struck out on his own and invented a machine to rival Edison's Kinetoscope. He called it the *Mutoscope,* another variation on the peep show, and formed a syndicate called the K.M.C.D. Group to develop and market it. The Mutoscope was built on the idea of the flip-book, which was simply a stack of photographs that reproduced the movement of the subject when flipped through rapidly. In the Mutoscope, the pictures, which were paper prints, were fastened to a central core in a cabinet and spun by a hand crank. The large paper photographs gave much higher quality images than the 35-millimeter film used in Edison's Kinetoscopes. And since the Mutoscope was operated by hand, the viewer could control the speed at which it ran. For these reasons, the Mutoscope eclipsed the Kinetoscope as the chief peep show attraction at amusement parks and arcades. It remained popular long into the era of projected movies. As with the Kinetoscope, some of Dickson's films were fairly racy by Victorian standards, and because of this the Mutoscope became known as the "What the Butler Saw" machine.

Although Dickson did well with this invention, he quickly realized that projected movies were forging ahead of the peep show format. So in short order he designed and built a projector called the *Biograph,* which had its first showing in Pittsburgh on September 14, 1896. The syndicate now became the American Mutoscope and Biograph Company,

This Mutoscope model was commonly used in arcades. The woman viewing it is Anna Held, a star of the musical stage and one of the first international celebrities. The American Mutoscope and Biograph Company hired her to advertise their products. LIBRARY OF CONGRESS, PRINTS AND PHOTOGRAPHS DIVISION

which was commonly known as "Biograph." Not to be outdone, in November 1896, the Edison Company came out with a new projector called the *Projecting Kinetoscope,* which displaced the Vitascope. The Biograph and Edison companies became the chief competitors in the American movie business during these early years.

THE AMERICAN MOVIE MACHINE GEARS UP

To keep up with all the peep shows and projectors that were grinding away in the mid-1890s, film production shifted into high gear. Most of the early films were what was called *actualities.* These were short documentary pictures, like the Lumières' first films, depicting scenes of everyday life, vaudeville acts, scenic places, well-known personalities, parades, military exercises, and sporting events. Trains were especially popular. Many film companies made their own versions of the Lumières' "The Train Coming into the Station," which had terrorized the audience at the Grand Café. Cavalry charges were another favorite. Any large object rushing directly at the camera was a sure bet to startle and excite the spectators.

As the movie business expanded, cameramen fanned out across the globe in search of new subjects. In 1897, the new head of Edison's Kinetoscope department, James White, traveled throughout the American West and Mexico, sponsored by railroad executives who saw films as a way to boost tourism. To satisfy his sponsors, White included in his films shots of railroad lines, hotels, and scenic attractions. The following year, White's travels took him to the Far East—to Japan, Hong Kong, and China.

In addition to actualities, short acted films were also popular. Most of these were comic sketches based on a simple gag or joke. In Biograph's *The Tramp and the Bather,* for example, a tramp steals the clothes of a man who is swimming in a lake. The bather swims ashore, squeezes into a handy barrel, and chases the tramp. In *The Bad Boy and Poor Old Grandpa,* a mischievous boy sneaks up behind an old man reading a newspaper and sets it on fire. The Tramp and the Bad Boy became regular characters in these little comedies.

COVERING THE NEWS: THE MOVIES GO TO WAR

In 1898, the Spanish-American War broke out, and motion pictures were launched into another important role: coverage of news events. Edison hired a man named William Paley as an independent licensee to cover the war. Paley traveled to Florida, where he filmed troop preparations in

A poster advertising a "camp-meeting" that featured, among many other things, films of the Spanish-American War, which at the time was also called the Cuban War.

At the MARTHA'S VINEYARD

Camp-Meeting Tabernacle.

Two Nights---THURSDAY and FRIDAY, August 3d and 4th.

Programme for August 3d. | ❋ | A SUPERB ENTERTAINMENT.

The Edison Vitagraph Co.,

MR. J. STUART BLACKTON, The Distinguished Cartoonist, Artist, Humorist & Monologuist,

And the Popular Entertainer, Shadowgraphist and Mimic. **MR. ALBERT E. SMITH,**

And the GREAT CUBAN WAR PICTURES.

We have just received from Mr. Edison's Cuban Representatives at Havana and Key West, Florida, a series of Thrilling Animated Pictures, taken especially for "The Edison Vitagraph." Events of Supreme Interest to all Americans at the present

WAR · CRISIS.

FUNERAL OF THE MAINE SAILORS AT HAVANA. Longest Film ever taken.

THE "MAINE" as she lay in Havana Habor, before the explosion.

Secretary of the Navy, LONG, and Captain SIGSBEE, Hero of the "Maine," at Navy Department, Washington.

Consul General LEE'S arrival at Washington.

American War Correspondents racing for cable office to send first news to United States.

The Battleship "MAINE" leaving Boston Harbor for Havana.

The Spanish Cruiser, **"VIZCAYA,"** entering New York Harbor.

Panoramic View of MORRO CASTLE, Entrance to Havana Harbor.

[The taking machine was located on the U. S. Dispatch boat, "Dolphin," and film was taken as the vessel rounded Morro Castle Point, leaving the Harbor.]

U. S. S. "INDIANA," Coaling at Sea, a wonderful picture.

Cruiser "NEW YORK" in a storm off the Coast of Cuba. (In this picture the taking camera was lashed to the deck during the terrible storm and shows the gigantic waves rolling towards and breaking against side of vessel.)

Heaving the Log on the Cruiser "NEW YORK" during the above storm. (Two sailors are seen at the stern performing this duty while the vessel rushes along at a high rate of speed.)

The Launch of a Steel War Vessel at San Francisco, Cal., and **50 other Wonderful and Interesting Subjects,** many comic, some startling, including all the latest popular American and Foreign Views.

Entire change of Program for second Evening. The most thrilling illustrated lecture of the age.

"WITH DEWEY AT MANILLA."

A story of the Glorious Victory as related by an eye-witness on board the Flagship Olympia, illustrated by Lantern Slides and

ACTUAL MOVING VITAGRAPH PICTURES,

taken on the spot

Showing the Great Ironclads in Action.

Tampa, as well as the burial of servicemen who had died in the explosion of the battleship *Maine* in Havana harbor in February 1898. He then accompanied the military to Cuba, filming the American fleet and troop movements. However, he was not able to film the action itself; cameramen were not allowed on the battlefield because it was deemed too dangerous to present a stationary target standing behind a large camera planted on a tripod. To make up for this, some of the key battles were reenacted for the camera on safer ground, back in New Jersey, using National Guard soldiers. Reenactments like this became a common way of reproducing news events that couldn't be filmed directly or that happened when cameras weren't there.

Edison Company photographers were making films of the Pan-American Exposition in Buffalo, New York, in 1901 when President William McKinley was assassinated. They turned their cameras on events following the assassination, including the funeral procession. The assassination itself was reenacted and filmed later in the studio.

These were the first newsreels, the films of current events that, along with cartoons, would serve as the opening act to feature films in movie theaters through the 1950s—until television brought the news home and made it a nightly event. ✳

··❧ 10 ❧··

From the Grand Café to the Moon

So we find ourselves back at the Grand Café on that December evening in 1895, the date that has gone down in history as the birthday of the movies. But when we think about all of the people who had been working for years toward this very end, Louis and Auguste Lumière seem to be unlikely candidates for the honor of being "the father of motion pictures." They were late entries into the motion-picture race. It was just a year earlier, in 1894, that Louis got the idea to get into the movie business when he saw a demonstration of Edison's Kinetoscope in Paris. So how was it that these newcomers managed to jump so quickly to the head of the line?

A FAMILY BUSINESS

The Lumières were successful businessmen, Europe's leading manufacturers of dry plates for still photography. Louis was the inventor in the family, the one who had discovered the new plate-making process. He had an inventive mind, and as soon as he saw the Kinetoscope films, he set out to design his own machine. He was also prodded by his father, Antoine, who saw immediately that the peep show format of Edison's

Louis and Auguste Lumière preparing to take a photograph.
Louis, on the left, is holding a camera. LIBRARY OF CONGRESS,
MOTION PICTURE, BROADCASTING, AND RECORDED SOUND DIVISION

Kinetoscope "box" was not the wave of the future. He told his son, "You can do better. Try to get the image out of the box."

It didn't take Louis long. By early 1895 he had designed a reversible camera; with minor changes it could be used as either a camera or projector. He called it the *Cinématographe,* and enlisted an engineer and close friend named Jules Carpentier to build it. The Cinématographe was a lightweight machine, less than twelve pounds, operated by a hand crank. It used a claw mechanism to drive perforated film through the projector with an intermittent movement. In contrast to Edison's bulky Kinetograph, which was confined to the studio, it was portable enough to film everyday life on the street.

By March 1895, Louis had a workable machine. He gave a private showing of some short films at an industrial meeting in Paris and another in June to a group of photographers in Lyons.

The Decision to Go Public

Oddly enough, it was not the brothers but their father, Antoine, who pushed for a public debut of the Cinématographe. He may very well be the one responsible for securing the Lumières' place in history. Antoine was the showman of the family, a painter and photographer and something of a free spirit. He was drawn to the bohemian world of the theater, the concert hall, and the café, whereas his sons were more stodgy, given to business and engineering. Unlike Louis, who declared that there was no future in film, Antoine was excited by its potential for entertainment. Louis and Auguste tended to look down on the world of actors and musicians as somewhat disrespectable, and preferred to keep the company of industrialists and professionals. In a letter to Jules Carpentier dated December 31, 1835, Louis wrote, "My father plagued us to let him organize the showings in Paris and we have tried not to involve ourselves in them at all." Carpentier agreed with Louis's point of view, actually discouraging him from going public. He thought of his work as a scientific achievement; a public show would drag it down to the level of common entertainment.

So it was Antoine who took care of arrangements for the December showing. He scouted locations, finally deciding on the Grand Café. He sent out announcements and acted as official greeter. The weather was bad in Paris that day, and only about thirty-five people paid the admission to see this historic screening. Nevertheless, the show was a great success. The short films of everyday scenes—like workers leaving a factory, a mother and father feeding a baby, and a train coming into a station—amazed the audience.

Word of this spectacular new entertainment spread throughout the city in no time, and soon the Lumières were putting on twenty shows a day to standing-room-only crowds. The Grand Café became the world's first movie theater open to paying audiences. People from all walks of life were eager to pay the small admission fee to see this latest marvel of nineteenth-century science.

Encouraged by their success, the Lumières expanded their operations, taking their show on the road to England, Belgium, Germany, and Holland. By 1897, they had taken the world by storm. They trained hundreds of franchise operators in the use of the Cinématographe and sent camera crews out to film events and places few people would ever be able to see on their own. Prints of these films were sold to exhibitors and were shown worldwide.

The success of the Lumières was meteoric but short-lived. Their last big presentation was at the Paris Exposition of 1900, where they projected films on a giant screen measuring seventy-nine feet high by ninety-nine feet wide. After that, they cut back on film production and concentrated on the manufacture and sales of their equipment. By final count, the Lumière brothers produced about 1,425 short films.

FRANCHISING THE CINÉMATOGRAPHE

In spite of the pressure of competition, Louis Lumière was slow to put the Cinématographe into commercial production. For one thing, he was a perfectionist, constantly making minor changes in the design, and he dragged his feet for months before finally giving Jules Carpentier the go-ahead to build the machines. As the year 1895 drew to a close, he wrote to Carpentier, "They are hot on our heels from all sides." Louis knew that to be competitive he had to get his invention on the market quickly, but he still kept dithering about whether to sell the machines outright or franchise them. Finally, he decided on franchising, which meant that he would retain ownership of the machines. Operators who wanted to buy their own would have to get them somewhere else. As a result, other inventors bypassed the Lumière patent and constructed their own machines— some of them superior to the Cinématographe. Louis changed his mind in 1897 and put his Cinématographes up for sale on the open market, but by that time the moment had passed. The Lumières were losing ground to others.

Among the spectators at the Grand Café was a man who would soon become famous for making movies of a very different kind. His name was Georges Méliès (1861–1938). He was a theatrical showman and magician. Méliès had used magic lantern projections as part of his magic show, but the Lumières' films were the first he had ever seen. He was impressed:

The other guests and I found ourselves in front of a small screen, similar to those we use for projections, and after a few minutes, a stationary photograph showing the Place Bellcour in Lyons was projected. A little surprised, I scarcely had time to say to my neighbour: "Have we been brought here to see projections? I've been doing these for ten years." No sooner had I stopped speaking when a horse pulling a cart started to walk towards us followed by other vehicles, then a passerby. In short, all the hustle and bustle of a street. We sat with our mouths open, without speaking, filled with amazement.

At this time, Georges Méliès was the owner of a theater in Paris called the Théâtre Robert-Houdin, where he staged magic acts and magic lantern shows. The acts ranged from coin and card tricks to complex illusions, such as making subjects appear and disappear or transforming them from one thing into another. Often, several illusions were strung together to form a short skit.

Méliès had always had a theatrical bent. As a child, he spent his time drawing, putting on puppet shows, and, later, learning and performing magic tricks. With this background, he was well prepared to apply his unique skills to film.

When he saw the Lumières' show, Méliès decided he had to have his own projector. The Lumières wouldn't sell him one since at that time they were only allowing franchises. So Méliès shopped around and discovered that an Englishman named Robert William Paul was marketing a projector called a *Theatrograph*. He bought one and immediately began screening short films in his theater. At first, he used films made by others—mostly from Edison's studio. But in short order, Méliès built and patented his own camera and began making films similar to the Lumières' short scenes from everyday life. His first film was nothing special—one minute of Méliès's brother Gaston and two friends playing cards in the garden.

A Lucky Accident

In 1896, the year after the Lumières' first show, Méliès made eighty films, mostly short travel and news features. There was nothing original about them that would suggest what was to come. Then one day a minor problem with his camera brought about a breakthrough. According to Méliès's account, it happened while he was filming on a Paris street. Here is how he described the incident in a later interview:

Georges Méliès. British Film Institute

My first camera was rudimentary. The film often tore or jammed and wouldn't run. One day when I was filming in the Place de l'Opéra, the film jammed. It took me a full minute to release the film and start the camera again. During this minute, passers by, buses, and automobiles had moved. On projecting the spliced film, I suddenly saw a carriage turn into a hearse, and men become women. The substitution trick, called the mid-shot trick, had been found.

This fortunate mishap gave Méliès the idea for his first *trick film*, as they came to be called. In the film, titled *The Vanishing Lady*, Méliès adapted for the screen a popular stage magician's technique called the substitution effect. Here's how it worked: with the camera running,

A scene from Méliès's *The Vanishing Lady,* showing the lady transformed into a skeleton. Bʀɪᴛɪꜱʜ Fɪʟᴍ Iɴꜱᴛɪᴛᴜᴛᴇ

Méliès sat an actress in a chair and covered her with a silk cloth. Then he stopped the camera, substituted a skeleton for the actress, replaced the cloth, and restarted the camera. Finally, he swept the cloth away and—*presto!*—the woman had been miraculously turned into a skeleton.

Méliès made many of these trick films. In them he made use of the same kinds of skits performed by magicians on the stage of the Théâtre Robert-Houdin—people and objects appearing and disappearing, or transforming from one thing to another.

GIANT BUGS AND FLOATING HEADS

Also in 1896, Méliès made the first film of a type that would later become known as the horror film. It was titled *A Terrible Night.* In this film, a guest at a hotel enters his room. As soon as he goes to bed he is attacked by huge bedbugs, which swarm over his bed and up the wall. The man frantically attacks and destroys the bugs with a broom.

Thus Méliès became the father of the popular oversized-insect-out-of-control movie, a standard variety of horror film to this day.

Méliès soon realized that to develop his ideas he would need greater control over the conditions under which his films were made. So in 1897, he built his own studio. It was much more complex and sophisticated than Edison's Black Maria, built in 1892. In contrast to Edison's tarpaper shack, it looked like a large, well-built greenhouse, with walls and a roof made of glass to allow the maximum amount of light. Most of his movies after 1896 were shot in this studio, where he could have complete control over every detail of filmmaking to create the kind of fantasy world he imagined.

One after the other, Méliès introduced new horror and fantasy effects. Devils and vampires, ghosts and floating heads paraded through his movies. He adapted ideas from the phantasmagoria to film and invented some new tricks of his own. In *The Bewitched Inn,* a traveler's clothes take on a life of their own and go prancing around. In *Four Troublesome Heads,* three of Méliès's own heads become detached from his body and float around the room. Méliès (at least his head) often appeared in his own films. He was really a one-man film production outfit. He wrote, directed, edited, designed sets, and acted. He even hand-colored some of his films frame by frame.

Drawing on his experience as a magician and lanternist, Méliès invented in short order many of the special effects that would become Hollywood standards. Here is how he described it:

> *I invented this special type of unusual shot which my clients called transformation shots. It would be more correct to say, fantasy shots. They were made with a series of techniques which could only be called "trick shots." By chance I had found a trick, stopping the camera, which permitted all kinds of substitutions. One trick would lead to another. I created fade-ins by double exposure to change sets, to make characters appear or disappear progressively. I also carried out apparitions, disappearances, and metamorphoses through double exposure on a black backdrop or black spaces in the set.*

Until the age of computer graphics, most modern special effects in films like *Star Wars* and *Superman* were accomplished using the same basic techniques developed by Méliès.

Like the early work of the Lumières and Edison and others, Méliès's first films were very short—fifteen to ninety seconds—and each one consisted of a single scene. The camera would be set up and the scene would be recorded until it ended or the camera ran out of film. The camera never moved. At this time every filmmaker used this same basic approach, whether it was Louis Lumière photographing on a Paris street

This 1897 poster advertises Harry Kellar, one of the most famous magicians of the nineteenth century. Decapitation had been a popular part of stage magicians' acts for many years, and it was a frequent theme in Méliès's movies. LIBRARY OF CONGRESS, PRINTS AND PHOTOGRAPHS DIVISION

or Thomas Edison filming a dancer in the Black Maria. There was no editing and no attempt to create a plot.

Then in 1899, Méliès made another major breakthrough. He became the first filmmaker to put together a longer story consisting of a sequence of connected scenes. It was a seven-minute adaptation of the story of *Cinderella,* told in twenty scenes with a cast of thirty-five characters. This was a big jump forward, but the movie was still limited by the single-scene approach. Each scene was photographed from a fixed camera position, and then the scenes were simply stitched together.

The acting in all of these films was purely pantomime. Without sound or subtitles, the story had to be told through action and gesture. As with all films produced at this time, any musical accompaniment was provided by the showmen who exhibited them, usually by a piano, organ, or small group of musicians.

Méliès continued to produce his trick films at a brisk pace. In 1901 alone, his company, Star Films, released twenty-nine of them. They became more elaborate as Méliès perfected his techniques. In *The One-Man Band,* for example, he used the technique of double exposure to create a group of seven musicians, all of them played by Méliès himself. Many of his films were full of the usual Méliès antics—devils, ghosts, decapitated heads, strange transformations, and so on. In *Tit for Tat, or a Good Joke with My Head,* several of Méliès's detached heads do battle with each other. And in *The Brahmin and the Butterfly,* a giant caterpillar emerges from its cocoon and turns into a butterfly woman.

A Trip to the Moon

There were hundreds of these short films, and a few longer ones, but the movie for which Méliès is most famous appeared in 1902. Titled *A Trip to the Moon,* it was loosely based on the stories of Jules Verne and H. G. Wells, whose tales of travel in space and time were the forerunners of modern science fiction. But Méliès gave the story his own wacky comic twist, poking fun at the many scientific societies that were flourishing at that time. These societies tended to be conservative, stuffy, and deadly serious. Since the film was silent, Méliès composed a script to be read along with it.

In the movie, Méliès plays the part of the president of the French Astronomical Society, a Professor Barbenfouillis, whose name means "whiskers in a tangle." As the film opens, the professor is madly scrawling diagrams on a blackboard as he explains his plan to explore the moon by having himself and a group of astronomers placed inside a "space shell" and shot out of a giant cannon. The plan is voted on and accepted, with the exception of one objector who is silenced by a barrage of books and papers from the hand of Barbenfouillis. So, to much fanfare, the cannon is forged and the party is launched on its journey.

When the shell reaches its destination, it lands smack in the eye of the man in the moon, an image that has become an icon in the world of filmmaking. As the explorers emerge from the shell, they are lashed by a snowstorm and scramble to find shelter in a crater, from which they descend into the interior of the moon. They enter a cave of giant mushrooms, where they are attacked by one of the moon creatures called Selenites. The professor strikes the creature, which immediately explodes into a cloud of dust. But more of them rush to the attack, and the party is captured and taken before the king. The professor saves the day, however, by lifting the king over his head and throwing him to the ground, which causes the king to explode. In the confusion, the astronauts escape, pursued by the Selenites.

The explorers find their shell and make their escape back to Earth, splashing down in the sea. The shell sinks to the bottom, giving everyone a chance to marvel at the strange wonders of the deep. Finally, the air

The most famous scene from Méliès's *A Trip to the Moon*. BRITISH FILM INSTITUTE

in the capsule floats it to the surface, and a passing steamship tows it to safety. Back in Paris, the crew is greeted with heroes' welcomes.

A Trip to the Moon was much longer and more complex in plot, characterization, and special effects than anything that had been done up to that time. Méliès took what he had learned from the short trick films and blended the effects with a coherent story line. The film brought Méliès international fame, and he followed it with several others based on space travel, fairy tales, and undersea voyages. But *A Trip to the Moon* is still considered his masterpiece. In it he combined imaginative storytelling with his trademark "trickery" and wry wit to create a landmark in the history of film. ✳

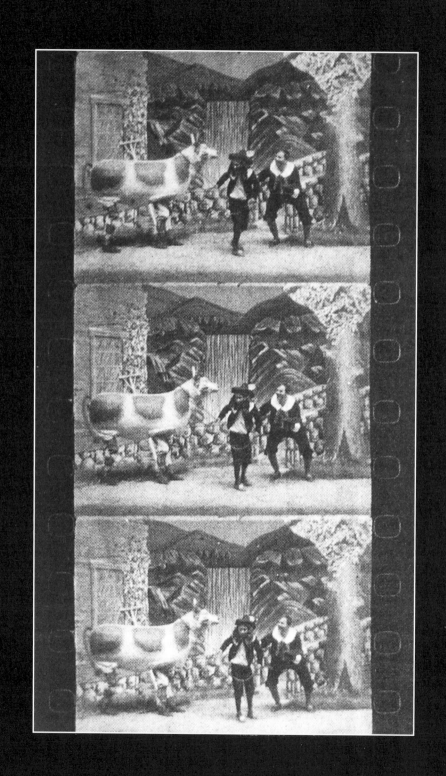

⋯≳ 11 ≲⋯
The Movies Tell Stories

In the United States and Europe, the novelty of actualities held audiences for a while. But like any flashy new invention, whether it's the latest video game or another rocket being fired into space, the novelty soon wore off. This happened to the movie industry in the final years of the nineteenth century. In fact, it got so bad that the producers of vaudeville shows in America took to putting films at the end of the program to prod spectators into leaving the theater quickly so a new crop of paying customers could be seated. It looked as if the doubters like Louis Lumière, who predicted that movies would be just a passing fad, might be right. But the doubters hadn't counted on the power of movies to invent worlds and tell stories.

In the early years of the twentieth century, the one-minute actualities evolved into longer, more complex documentaries, and the short acted skits grew into longer story films. Méliès's *A Trip to the Moon* had been a resounding success, and other filmmakers quickly followed his lead. Productions ran the gamut from stories like *Jack and the Beanstalk* (1902) to informative documentaries such as *The Life of an American Fireman* (1903).

Three frames from Edwin S. Porter's story film *Jack and the Beanstalk*.

In 1903, a director at Edison studios named Edwin S. Porter made a film that broke the mold of earlier movies. It was called *The Great Train Robbery,* and it was the first western ever made. As the movie opens, a gang of bandits overpowers and ties up a stationmaster at a railroad telegraph office, then sneaks aboard a train that has stopped to take on water. The train departs, and farther down the track the robbers force the engineer to stop it. They steal the payroll, rob the passengers, and make their escape. But a posse is mobilized and the gang is finally hunted down.

The Great Train Robbery ran for about ten minutes and consisted of fourteen scenes. By modern standards it looks pretty primitive. Most scenes are filmed in the usual way—a single shot with the camera planted in a fixed position at eye level. Nevertheless, to audiences at the time the film was a revelation. It cut back and forth from events on the train to

The final shot from *The Great Train Robbery* is a close-up of one of the robbers shooting his pistol directly into the camera. Both the close-up and the direct confrontation with the viewer were startling innovations for the time. EDISON NATIONAL HISTORIC SITE

action happening at the same time in the telegraph office, and later to a dance hall where the stationmaster, freed by his daughter, brings word of the robbery and musters men for a posse. In another scene, a camera is placed on top of the speeding train to film a fight. And as the robbers escape through the woods, the camera is freed from its fixed position and pans with, or follows, the action. The grand finale is a startling close-up of one of the outlaws firing six shots directly into the camera.

By 1903, story films accounted for about forty percent of the Edison Company's output and a good share of Biograph's and other American and European companies' as well. It was the growing ability of films to tell stories that saved the day for the movies.

SOUND AND THE SILENTS

Movies made before the coming of synchronized sound are called *silent* movies. If that label gives the impression that there was no sound with these films, it couldn't be more wrong. There was plenty. Sound was provided by the exhibitors, however, not by the filmmakers. Music might be furnished by a pianist or a small orchestra, or several kinds of mechanical music machines, such as phonographs, player pianos, and organs. There was also a good deal of noise supplied by sound effects. As a reviewer for the *Philadelphia Record* reported in 1897, "At the Bijou the roar of the waves, splashing of water, the playing of bands of music, a locomotive whistle, bell, stream, etc., are accompaniments that have played no small share in the 48 weeks' success of the biograph."

Another source of sound was the lecturer, or "talker," who narrated or explained the film as it was running. This was a natural addition to educational and travel films, but it also became necessary with some of the longer story films. A common complaint about many of the early story films was that they were confusing. Directors and editors had not yet learned how to photograph and edit action so that the story made sense

FILM BY THE FOOT

In the early years of motion pictures, the price of a film depended on its length; films sold for about ten cents per foot. Until around 1900, one limitation on the running time of a movie was the length of film stock available. The fifty-foot length (about one minute of film) was all filmmakers could get for several years. That was the size set by Edison's Kinetoscope. In addition, the Eastman Company, which made most of the film stock, was more interested in making film for the booming amateur photography market than for movies. So the short film dominated until public interest waned and Méliès and Porter and others began making their story films. The film for *The Great Train Robbery* was 740 feet long. By 1905, the thousand-foot "one-reel" movie had became the standard.

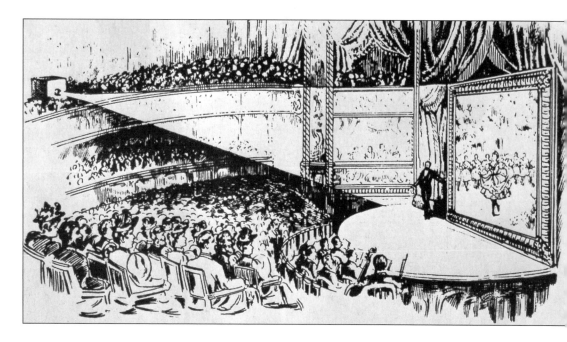

to the audiences. The viewers couldn't follow the plot, so talkers were hired to explain it. Other theater operators put actors behind the screen to fill in the spoken parts.

Movies with synchronized sound were still a long way off; the first feature film with recorded sound was *The Jazz Singer,* which opened in 1927. But Thomas Edison dreamed of combining sound and pictures from the very beginning of his interest in film, and he started William Dickson working on the problem in 1889. Six years later, Dickson made the first experimental sound film of a man (probably Dickson himself) playing the violin into a phonograph horn while two other men danced. This idea led to another Edison-Dickson invention called the *Kineto-phone,* which was a Kinetoscope with a phonograph inside the cabinet. The customer would watch the film through the peephole while listening to the sound accompaniment through a set of primitive earphones—rubber tubes connected to the phonograph.

In 1913, Edison introduced a version of the Kinetophone that com-

bined recorded sound with a film projected on a screen. He made nineteen talking pictures that year, but the results were disappointing. Modern movies have a sound track on the film, so sound and image are synchronized as they run through the projector together. Edison was still using a separate phonograph connected to the projector by a belt, and the synchronization of sound and picture often broke down. This resulted in the annoying effect of an actor's lips appearing to say one thing while the sound said something else. Audiences didn't respond well to this invention, and Edison soon abandoned it.

Another way of using film to tell stories with music was introduced by Edison in 1899—the *story-song*. A singer performed songs while the movie played, and the lyrics told the story. One typical example, called *Love and War,* was the story of a hero during the Spanish-American War who falls in love with a Red Cross nurse, gets promoted from private to captain, and returns home in triumph. When exhibitors ordered one of these films, they also received the music and lyrics to be performed with it. There were six songs with *Love and War.* Story-songs became a regular part of early film shows.

THE MOVIES FIND A HOME

A great leap forward in the history of the movies took place in 1905 in Pittsburgh, Pennsylvania. Two brothers, Harry and John Harris, opened a theater devoted exclusively to showing films. They charged a nickel admission and called the theater the *Nickelodeon.* It was an instant success. An article in the magazine *The Moving Picture World* on May 4, 1907, had this to say:

> *The nickel place of amusement made its appearance with no greater blare of trumpets than the noise of its phonograph horn and the throaty persuasions of its barker. . . . It is multiplying faster than guinea pigs, and within a few months has attained to that importance where we may no longer snub it as one of the catch-pennies of the street.*

Films now had a home, and the movie business had changed overnight. Nickelodeons were soon springing up all over the country,

making cheap entertainment available to working-class people. By 1910, there were more than ten thousand of them in the United States.

Nickelodeons were called the poor-man's theater. The more luxurious vaudeville theaters and opera houses charged higher admission and attracted a middle- and upper-class audience. But most workers could afford a nickel, and it became common for the whole family, squalling babies and all, to spend an afternoon or evening at the movies. The quality

A nickelodeon theater front.
LIBRARY OF CONGRESS, PRINTS AND PHOTOGRAPHS DIVISION

The Nickelodeon and the Reformers

Social reformers soon became concerned about the effect of nickelodeon theaters on public morals. For one thing, movie theaters were—and remain—popular with couples. The idea that a lower-class crowd, many of them questionable "foreigners," was gathered in a dark theater doing who knows what made some people uneasy. But the movies themselves also fell under scrutiny. Reformers at the beginning of the twentieth century held that all art, literature, and popular entertainment should be morally uplifting. They were especially troubled because women and children made up a good part of the nickelodeon audience.

At first, French filmmakers were particularly suspect, because they dealt with the all-time favorite movie themes, sex and violence, more frankly than the Americans. Soon even the many short comic films made in America that turned on a slightly "naughty" joke began to disappear as pressure was exerted on theater operators to clean up their act. To this end, film companies turned to the classics of literature for material: Shakespeare's plays and the works of such writers as Charles Dickens and Nathaniel Hawthorne.

of nickelodeons varied a great deal from place to place. So did the audiences. At their best, these theaters were plain, simple buildings with few amenities. At their worst, in the poor neighborhoods of large cities, they were dirty, crowded, noisy, and foul smelling. Patrons spit on the floor and littered it with peanut shells. Diseases spread easily in the stuffy, cramped confines of these places, and health authorities frequently tried to bar children from them. But neighborhood theaters drew people together, and going to the movies provided an opportunity for socializing. Newly arrived immigrants also found the nickelodeons to be a welcome source of entertainment, since the movies were silent and most immigrants were not only poor but also didn't speak English.

According to the article, here is what you needed to start a nickelodeon:

One storeroom seating from 200 to 500 persons
One phonograph with extra large horn
One young woman cashier
One electric sign
One cinematograph, with operator
One canvas on which to throw the pictures
One piano
One barker
One manager
As many chairs as the store will hold
A few brains and a little tact

Toward Hollywood

With the advent of the nickelodeon, the demand for movies skyrocketed. Exhibitors needed a constant supply of new films. Production companies sprang up across the United States, and French and English imports poured into the country. The Edison Company faced plenty of

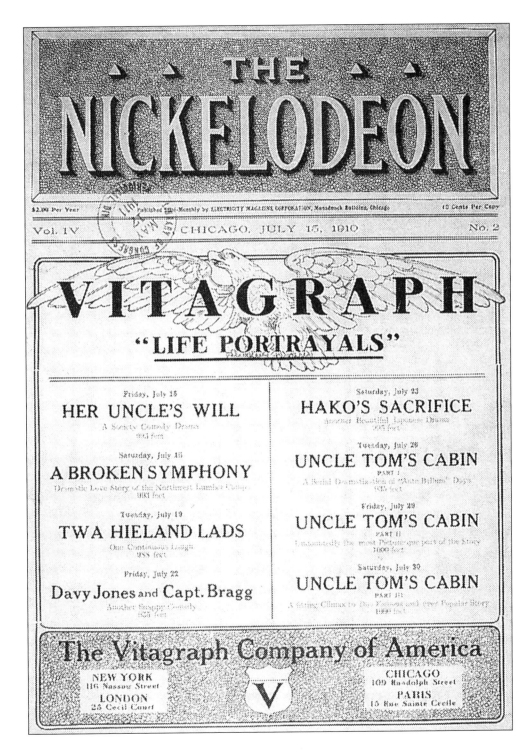

An ad from *The Nickelodeon* magazine, 1910, for a Vitagraph show featuring story films. Films were usually changed daily, except for those that were especially popular, like *Uncle Tom's Cabin*. LIBRARY OF CONGRESS, PRINTS AND PHOTOGRAPHS DIVISION

competition from home and from abroad. Public taste changed rapidly, and production companies that didn't keep up soon failed. Audiences were becoming more demanding, no longer awed by the simple wonder of moving images. To keep people coming to the movies, photographers, directors, and editors had to develop new ways of using the camera and linking scenes together to create more interesting and coherent stories. And they did.

That's not to say that a lot of junk wasn't cranked out in haste to feed the insatiable public appetite for movies. Films were sold to exhibitors by the foot no matter what the movie might be. Nickelodeon operators needed a constant supply of new films and audiences still weren't all that picky about what they watched, so there wasn't a huge incentive to strive for quality. Nevertheless, this frenzy of production served as a training

A photo postcard of the Christie Studios on the northwest corner of Sunset Boulevard and Gower in Hollywood, from the 1920s. The original studio built on this site, in 1911, was called Nestor Comedies. A plaque on the flagpole now marks the location as the First Motion Picture Studio in Hollywood. TOMMY DANGCIL

ground for hundreds of cameramen, directors, and editors, and some good work came out of it.

It was a heady atmosphere, full of excitement and discovery, but it was also fiercely competitive. According to one account, in 1898 there were 109 different machines for taking and projecting motion pictures. The inventiveness of their designs was equaled only by the inventiveness of their names. There were the Luminograph, the Badizographe, the Lapiposcope, the Phototachygraphe, the Muscularscope, the Mimimoscope, the Mouvementoscope, the Chronovivographe, the Klondikoscope, the Cinographoscope (getting both "-graph" and "-scope" into the name), and a host of others.

Fall behind in this free-for-all, and you were out.

Around 1909, the Edison Company began to decline. Its movies failed to keep up with new methods of filming and editing that were being pioneered by other film companies, both in America and in Europe. At one point, Edison considered selling out to the Biograph Company but reconsidered and kept going, with varying degrees of success over the next few years.

In 1918, Edison left the movie business to others and turned his amazingly fertile mind to the huge array of experiments that were under way at his labs in West Orange—flying machines, electric cars, X-rays, storage batteries, and dozens of others. By 1920, the operation at West Orange was an industrial complex employing ten thousand workers in its factories and laboratories. Film was just one part of a sprawling octopus of experiment and invention.

By the time Edison left the movies, the movies had already left Edison. The center had shifted. The East Coast was no longer the hub of the movie business in America. Filmmakers had begun building their studios and telling their stories in a sunny little town near Los Angeles in Southern California. It was called Hollywood. ✷

Afterword

The pioneers of the first films—the Lumières, Thomas Edison, Georges Méliès—lived to see the movies grow from a few grainy snippets of ordinary life shown in the basement of a French café to a multimillion-dollar industry. In 1938, the year Georges Méliès died, Americans bought eighty million tickets to the movies every week. There was hardly a town without at least one moving picture theater. The country was in the midst of a terrible depression, but people were flocking to the movies in droves to see the new crop of American idols: Humphrey Bogart, Bette Davis, Fred Astaire and Ginger Rogers, Cary Grant, Jeanette MacDonald, Mae West, Charlie Chaplin, the Marx Brothers. . . . The list goes on and on.

Much had changed since the invention of the movies, but through it all there was something for everyone. At first there were no permanent movie theaters, so films were shown in all sorts of places. For working-class people in cities and large towns there were abandoned stores hastily outfitted with a few wooden benches and a sheet draped over a line for a screen. And traveling showmen, like the itinerant lanternists before them, took the magic of the moving image out to the small towns. They turned meeting halls, theaters, and churches into temporary movie houses. At circuses and carnivals they set up tents painted black to darken them, and families sat on the ground to enjoy a mixed bag of short films. After 1905, the nickelodeons catered to audiences made up mostly of blue-collar working families and immigrants. Though it was not uncommon for people from the middle and upper classes to sneak over to the other side of the tracks for an evening's amusement, the upper classes generally preferred to watch their movies in the plush surroundings of vaudeville theaters and music halls, where films were shown along with variety acts: singers, dancers, comedians, jugglers, acrobats, magicians, and dancing bears.

But as films became longer and better made, a new type of theater appeared that attracted audiences willing and able to put up more than a nickel admission. These theaters were a far cry from the nickelodeons. They were known as *movie palaces,* and they lived up to the name. They were furnished with thick carpeting and luxurious seats, and the walls were plastered with ornate carvings and copies of Greek sculptures. Marble, polished wood, and large mirrors contributed to the atmosphere of elegance. Ushers in silk uniforms that matched the carpets and walls escorted the customers to their seats.

These movie palaces began to appear about the same time as full-length feature films. The first one, called the Strand, opened on Broadway in New York City in 1914, just as D. W. Griffith was making his three-hour epic, *The Birth of a Nation.* The Strand seated 3,300 people. Films, audiences, and theaters grew up together.

In the early days of film, the names of the actors weren't even mentioned. They were just workers, often hired by the day, often unemployed stage and vaudeville performers. The practice of not naming the actors in films continued until around 1912. But moviegoers wanted to know about the people they were seeing on the screen. Letters poured into the studios from fans asking for the names of their favorite actors and requesting photographs. This demand led to the creation of a new approach to movie making and marketing called "the star system." The studios began to focus on promoting the fame of movie stars as a way of drawing audiences to their films. They signed popular actors to long-term contracts and in many instances designed movies especially to showcase their stars. The star system began to emerge in 1910, when the Independent Motion Picture Company (known as Imp) staged a publicity stunt on behalf of actress Florence Lawrence. The owner of Imp, Carl Laemmle, had lured her away from Biograph with the promise of more money and greater public recognition. Soon after, nameless actors were transformed into movie stars and became the most important ingredient in motion pictures. In short order, the ancestors of the modern fan magazine sprang up, and entrepreneurs soon discovered that fans would pay for practically anything with a picture of their favorite actor on it.

Another big change in the first few decades of the twentieth century was the development of a "language" of film. At first, no one knew how to tell a story with film. They were making it up as they went along. As often happens, a new medium starts out by borrowing from an older, familiar form. So it was natural that the first story films, like those of Georges Méliès, adopted the model of the theater: the camera was planted in front of the stage like a spectator at a play, and it stayed there while actors played their parts.

If you compare this with the look of modern movies, you'll see that the art of filmmaking has come a long way. (Next time you watch a movie, notice how long the camera stays fixed on a single shot. It's hardly ever more than a few seconds.) Step by step, early filmmakers learned how to vary shots, link scenes, and edit (cut) the film.

By the mid-1930s, movies with complicated plots, fully developed characters, and sophisticated use of camera and editing were being turned out regularly by giant corporate studios. Film was still black-and-white, but synchronized sound had been around for a decade and movie stars had become national icons.

Today, we have grown used to razor-sharp pictures, true-to-life color, and Dolby surround sound. We hardly even notice effects that would have seemed impossible to audiences a century ago: sudden jump cuts from one scene to another, zooming lenses, extreme close-ups, flashbacks, cameras mounted on helicopters. Not to mention the explosions and flying bodies and surreal landscapes dished up courtesy of the modern special effects department.

The story of the moving image has taken us from a time when people saw scarcely any pictures to a time when we can hardly get away from them. Each step of the way, the makers of moving pictures have held audiences spellbound with new ways of creating their fictional worlds. At first the simple fact of a projected image on a wall was enough to both enchant and horrify. Then the picture was made to move, through the cunning artistry of lantern slides. Next came the flying ghosts of the phantasmagoria, giant moving panoramas and dioramas, zoetropes and praxinoscopes with their endless twirling and jumping, Muybridge's galloping horses, Marey's birds, and finally—the movies.

Now, a little more than a hundred years later, our world has become so saturated with moving pictures that they are almost like a fact of nature—always there, always have been. We take movies home on shining silver discs and watch them in our living rooms, in our cars, or anywhere we want on laptop computers and portable DVD players. Digital technology has taken the movies over another threshold, possibly even more revolutionary than the shift from glass slides to film. These days it's the magicians of the digital age who seek to enchant us. Their virtual worlds are so fantastically real it's hard to believe they exist only in the strange runes of computer code.

Imagine a man strolling down a modern city street. He passes a shop where a basketball game is playing on a TV in the window. He stops for a minute to watch, to see how the game is going. It looks like an L.A. Lakers game—tall people in yellow uniforms driving and leaping and slam-dunking. But after a few seconds the man shakes his head, as if to shake himself awake, and moves on. It has suddenly dawned on him that these are not the real Lakers. They aren't even real people. They're nothing but animated characters in a video game!

Maybe even in this been-there-done-that twenty-first century, it still *is* possible to experience a taste of what the audience at the Grand Café felt the first time a photograph suddenly sprang to life before their unsuspecting eyes. ✳

Timeline

1420 **The first known illustration of a camera obscura appears in a book by Johannes de Fontana.**

1492 Christopher Columbus sails from Spain to the island of Hispaniola in the West Indies.

1500 **Leonardo da Vinci describes the camera obscura in detail. However, he writes the description backward, as you would see it in a mirror, and it is not deciphered for almost 300 years.**

1543 Nicolaus Copernicus asserts that the planets, including the earth, circle a stationary sun. This is contrary to the prevailing belief that the planets, moon, sun, and stars circle the earth.

1558 **Giovanni Battista della Porta describes the camera obscura and how it can be used in his *Magia naturalis*.**

1609 Galileo uses a telescope he has constructed to observe the mountains and craters on the moon, and he discovers the four largest satellites of Jupiter.

1620 The *Mayflower* arrives at Cape Cod, November 11, bringing the first pilgrims from England to North America.

1646 **Athanasius Kircher publishes his *Ars magna lucis et umbrae* (The great art of light and shadow), in which he describes a room-size camera obscura and several other optical devices.**

1656 **Christiaan Huygens builds the first known magic lantern.**

1658 **Thomas Walgensten begins commercial production of the magic lantern.**

1671 **The second edition of Kircher's *Ars magna* includes a drawing of a magic lantern in operation.**

1687 Isaac Newton publishes his principle of universal gravitation, which demonstrates the mathematical basis for the attraction of any object to another.

1692 Dozens of women accused of witchcraft are brought to trial in Salem, Massachusetts. Twenty are executed in the next two years.

1769 James Watt introduces an improved version of the steam engine, ushering in the Industrial Revolution in England.

1776 The American Declaration of Independence is signed on July 4.

1787 Robert Barker is granted a patent for his panoramas. The first public presentation is given at Leicester Square, London, in 1792.

1789 The French Revolution begins, resulting in the overthrow of the monarchy in France.

1797 Etienne-Gaspard Robert (Robertson) presents his first phantasmagoria in a Capuchin convent in Paris. Two years later he applies for a patent for his Fantascope, a magic lantern on wheels.

1800 British chemist Sir Humphry Davy invents the arc lamp, which provides much brighter illumination than anything before.

1804 Ordered by President Thomas Jefferson, an expedition led by Meriwether Lewis and William Clark sets out from St. Louis, Missouri, to explore the newly acquired Louisiana Purchase. Their journey takes them across the continent to the Pacific Coast.

1822 Louis-Jacques-Mandé Daguerre and his partner Charles Bouton open the first diorama in Paris.

1824 Peter Mark Roget presents his paper on the persistence of vision to the British Royal Society.

1825 On September 27, the first steam railroad begins operation in England between Stockton and Darlington.

1826 Joseph Nicéphore Niepce uses a camera obscura to produce the first photograph—an image on paper that is permanently fixed. The thaumatrope is invented; credit is claimed by several people.

1832 Joseph Antoine Ferdinand Plateau constructs the first phenakistiscope.

1839 Louis-Jacques-Mandé Daguerre announces that he has invented a process for making photographs using the camera obscura. "Daguerreotypes," small images on metal plates, become the first practical type of photograph.

1859 Charles Darwin publishes *The Origin of Species,* in which he makes the controversial claim that species evolve through a process of natural selection.

1861 Abraham Lincoln becomes president of the United States.
The American Civil War begins.

1869 The last spike completing the transcontinental railroad, which connects the east and west coasts of the United States, is driven at Promontory, Utah, May 10.

1872/3 Eadweard Muybridge photographs Leland Stanford's horse Occident in motion.

1874 Pierre Janssen invents the photographic revolver to take a series of photographs on a phenakistiscope type of disk. He uses this machine to photograph the passage of Venus across the sun.

1877 Emile Reynaud patents the praxinoscope, an improved version of the zoetrope. Thomas Edison files for a patent for the first phonograph.

1881 Eadweard Muybridge and Etienne-Jules Marey meet in Paris. This meeting inspires Marey to begin investigating the use of photography in his work.

1882 Etienne-Jules Marey invents the photographic rifle, capable of taking twelve pictures per second on a disk.

1885 George Eastman produces the first commercial film, a celluloid emulsion on a paper base.

1888 Emile Reynaud is granted a patent in France for the use of perforations on strips of hand-drawn animated pictures.
Some evidence suggests that Louis Le Prince makes his first movies on sensitized paper strips.
Etienne-Jules Marey demonstrates his chronophotographic projector.
George Eastman places his first Kodak camera on the market.
Thomas Edison and Eadweard Muybridge meet to discuss combining Muybridge's zoöpraxiscope and Edison's phonograph to produce films with sound.

1891 George Eastman introduces the first commercially produced perforated film.
William Dickson and Thomas Edison patent the Kinetoscope.

1895 On November 1, Max Skladanowsky shows his films in Berlin.
On December 28, the Lumière brothers show their films to a paying audience at the Grand Café in Paris.

1896 **Georges Méliès makes the first of his trick films.**

1898 The Spanish-American War breaks out.
William Paley, working for the Edison Company, goes to Florida and Cuba to film the troops—the first major news coverage in films.

1901 American President William McKinley is assassinated at the Pan-American Exposition in Buffalo, New York. **A reenactment of the event is filmed by Edison Company photographers who were covering the exposition.**

1902 **Edwin S. Porter makes the film *The Life of an American Fireman*. Georges Méliès makes *A Trip to the Moon*, the first science-fiction movie.**

1903 **Edwin S. Porter makes *The Great Train Robbery*, the first western.**

1905 **The first nickelodeon opens in Pittsburgh, Pennsylvania.**

1911 **The Nestor Company opens the first film studio in Hollywood, California.**

1914 The assassination of Archduke Ferdinand of Austria triggers World War I.
The first "movie palace," the Strand, opens in New York City.

1915 **D. W. Griffith debuts his three-hour epic, *The Birth of a Nation*.**

Source Notes

All cited books, websites, and videos appear in the Bibliography.

1 A Beam of Light in a Darkened Room

pages 2–3. The description of Giovanni della Porta's camera obscura is based on della Porta's own description, quoted in David Robinson's essay "Realizing the Vision: 300 Years of Cinematography" in *Cinema: The Beginnings and the Future,* ed. Christopher Williams, p. 29. The description also draws on information from a website created by Dr. Robert Leggat, **A History of Photography**; the "Camera Obscura" chapter. www.rleggat.com/photohistory/history/cameraob.htm

page 5. The Oliver Sacks quotation is from his autobiographical book, *Uncle Tungsten: Memories of a Chemical Boyhood,* p. 154.

pages 8–9. The quotations from Daniel Barbaro and Algarotti are also from Robert Leggat's website. www.rleggat.com/photohistory/history/cameraob.htm

2 The Magic Lantern

pages 14–15. The quote from Christiaan Huygens ("for representation by means") and the description of his skeleton slides are from Laurent Mannoni, *The Great Art of Light and Shadow: Archaeology of the Cinema,* p. 38.

page 19. Kircher's explanation of producing movement by using cutout figures ("Out of natural paper make effigies") is from his *Ars Magna,* p. 794, quoted in Charles Musser, *The Emergence of Cinema: The American Screen to 1907,* p. 18.

page 19. Kircher's remarks about his catoptric lamp are from *Ars Magna,* p. 768, quoted in Musser, p. 20.

page 25. Charles Patin's description of a magic lantern show ("It seemed to me") is quoted in Mannoni, p. 60.

pages 27, 29. The quotations from the Peck and Snyder catalog ("The moving effects produced on the screen," "A scene painted on fixed glass," and "It is a great mystery") are from the website **The Dead Media Project.** www.deadmedia.org

page 27. The description of the "windmill with turning sails" by Petrus van Musschenbroek is quoted in Mannoni, p. 203.

3 The Lantern of Fear

pages 33–34. The unknown spectator's account of a séance is quoted in Mannoni, p. 139.

page 36. The viewer's description of images thrown into smoke ("That which appears extraordinary") is quoted in Mannoni, p. 139.

page 37. The account of Philidor's phantasmagoria ("The hysterical scream") is quoted in Marina Warner et al., *Tony Oursler: The Influence Machine*, p. 75.

page 40. The 1802 playbill ("This SPECTROLOGY") was quoted in the June 1998 issue of *Church History,* and can be found online at **The Material History of American Religion Project** in an article titled "From Demon Possession to Magic Show: Ventriloquism, Religion, and the Enlightenment." As the title suggests, this article gives considerable attention to the place of ventriloquism in the phantasmagoria. www.materialreligion.org/journal/magic.html

page 41. Robertson's opening "scientific" lecture is from his *Mémoires,* vol. 1, pp. 278-79, quoted in Musser, p. 24.

page 44. The scenario for *Preparation for the Sabbath* is quoted in Mannoni, p. 163.

page 44. Robertson's remark about the spread of the phantasmagoria ("There was not a quay") is quoted in Mervyn Heard's essay "The Magic Lantern's Wild Years," which is included in *Cinema: The Beginnings and the Future,* ed. Christopher Williams p. 33.

pages 44-45. The court's judgment against Robertson (these shows "serve only to capture the admiration") is quoted in Mannoni, p. 171.

4 ARTISTS OF THE BIG SCREEN

page 52. The story of Robert Barker's discovery of the panorama effect, as well as an interesting collection of writings about the panorama and other -ramas, can be found on Dr. Russell Naughton's website **Adventures in Cybersound.** www.acmi.net.au/AIC/PANORAMA.html

pages 61-62. The description of Daguerre's diorama of Canterbury Cathedral is quoted in **Adventures in Cybersound.** www.acmi.net.au/AIC/DAGUERRE_BIO.html For additional contemporary descriptions and expressions of amazement, see Helmut and Alison Gernsheim's book *L.J.M. Daguerre: The History of the Diorama and the Daguerreotype.* Also, a nice collection of writings and images related to the diorama can be found online at Derek Wood's website, **Midley History of Photography.** www.midleykent.fsnet.co.uk

page 64. The guidebook description of the Cosmorama is from *Mogg's New Picture of London and Visitor's Guide to Its Sights,* 1844. This and other contemporary reports and reviews, along with interesting pieces about many aspects of Victorian life, can be found on the website **The Victorian Dictionary.** www.victorianlondon.org

5 TOYS TO TEASE THE EYE

page 70. Leonardo da Vinci's comment that if you rapidly wave a lighted torch, "its whole course will seem a ring of flame" is quoted in Mannoni, p. 203.

page 75. The Sears catalog listing of children's magic lanterns can be found online at **The Dead Media Project.** www.deadmedia.org

6 THE MAGIC LANTERN MEETS THE PHOTOGRAPH

page 83. Louis du Hauron's comment about the possibility of reproducing motion with photography ("an apparatus designed to reproduce") and the text from his patent application ("The observer will believe") is quoted on Paul T. Burns's website, **The Complete History of the Discovery of Cinematography.** www.precinemahistory.net

page 84. The excerpt from *Art-Journal* about the Langenheim brothers' glass lantern slides ("The new magic-lantern pictures on glass") is quoted in Musser, pp. 29–30.

page 84. The Langenheim program ("1. Views of Niagara Falls") is from an 1852 broadside and is quoted in Musser, p. 30. Musser cites Sipley, "The Magic Lantern," p. 42.

page 85. The comment by the *New York Tribune* reviewer ("The dead appear almost to speak") is quoted in Musser, p. 31.

page 85. The article from *Magic Lantern* ("the old-fashioned, spasmodic, hitchy way") is quoted in Musser, p. 37.

pages 86–87. Muybridge's description of the wet-plate collodion process ("The problem ... was") is from the introduction to his *Animals in Motion* (1899), p. 13. It is quoted in Robert Bartlett Haas's *Muybridge: Man in Motion*, p. 48.

page 89. The *Alta California* account of Muybridge's setup to photograph Occident and his solution to the shutter problem ("On the third day") are quoted in Beaumont Newhall's *The History of Photography from 1839 to the Present Day*, p. 84.

pages 91–92. The report of the horse Abe Edgington's run in the *Pacific Rural Press* ("[Abe Edgington] came down the track in splendid style") is quoted in Haas, p. 110.

pages 92-94. Etienne Marey's letter to *La Nature* praising Muybridge's work ("What beautiful zoetropes he [Muybridge] could give us") is quoted in Gordon Hendricks's *Eadweard Muybridge: The Father of the Motion Picture*, p. 112.

7 ETIENNE-JULES MAREY AND THE FIRST TRUE FILMS

page 98. Marey's explanation of his thinking about graphic instruments ("Not only are these instruments") is quoted in Braun, *Picturing Time*, p. 40.

page 100. Marey's comment on the use of the zoetrope to animate drawings of a running horse ("These pictures placed in the instrument") is quoted in Mannoni, p. 325.

page 101. The excerpt from Marey's letter to the editor of *La Nature* ("I was dreaming of a kind of photographic gun") is quoted in Braun, p. 47.

page 101. Marey's statement that Muybridge's method can't be applied to the flight of birds ("it is not possible to apply") is quoted in Mannoni, p. 331.

page 105. The remark by the Paris City Council member ("One may study scientifically") is quoted in Mannoni, p. 335.

page 107. Marey's announcement to the French Academy of Sciences ("I hope to obtain a series of images") is quoted in Mannoni, p. 341.

page 108. Marey's description of the advantages of having a portable camera ("Using this method, one may operate") is quoted in Mannoni, p. 344.

page 109. Marey's letter to Demeny about the difficulty of projection ("My projection apparatus is proceeding") is quoted in Mannoni, p. 351.

8 THE RUSH TO THE MOVIES

page 115. The response of the "experts" to Donisthorpe's attempts to obtain financial backing (the idea was "wild, visionary") is quoted on the website **Who's Who of Victorian Cinema. www.victorian-cinema.net/newnes.htm**

pages 117-18. The excerpt from Reynaud's patent for the Théâtre Optique ("The aim of this device") is quoted in Mannoni, p. 371.

9 THOMAS EDISON AND THE AMERICAN MOVIE MACHINE

page 125. Thomas Edison's remark that the Kinetoscope would "do for the eye what the phonograph did for the ear" is quoted in Musser, p. 64 (and in many other places).

page 127. The report on the viewing of the Kinetoscope by the group from the Federation of Women's Clubs is from *Photogram,* May 1891, pp. 122–23; quoted in Musser, p. 68.

10 FROM THE GRAND CAFÉ TO THE MOON

page 140. Antoine Lumière's remark ("You can do better") is quoted on the website **CineScene** in an essay by Chris Dashiell titled "The Oldest Movies." www.cinescene.com/dash/lumiere.html

page 140. The letter from Louis Lumière to Jules Carpentier ("My father plagued us") is quoted in Mannoni, p. 459.

page 142. Méliès's account of his reaction to the Lumières' first show ("The other guests and I found ourselves") is quoted in an online biography of Méliès on **The Missing Link** website. To find the Méliès biography, click on "Features" at the home page, then on "Georges Méliès biography." www.mshepley.btinternet.co.uk

page 143. Méliès's account of his discovery of the substitution effect ("My camera was rudimentary") is transcribed from the film *The Magic of Méliès.*

page 146. Méliès's discussion of his trick shots ("I invented this special type") is transcribed from the film *The Magic of Méliès.*

11 THE MOVIES TELL STORIES

page 155. The report from the *Philadelphia Record* about the show at the Bijou ("At the Bijou the roar of the waves") is quoted in Musser, p. 178.

page 158. The complete story-song *Love and War* can be found online at **The Library of Congress American Memory Collections site, "Inventing Entertainment: The Early Motion Pictures and Sound Recordings of the Edison Companies."** http://memory.loc.gov.ammem/edhtml/edhome.html

page 158. The notice in *Moving Picture World* ("The nickel place of amusement") is quoted in Thomas W. Bohn and Richard L. Stromgren, *Light and Shadows: A History of Motion Pictures*, pp. 21–23. This article also includes the list of ingredients for a 5-cent theater.

Bibliography

Note: Books and websites marked with an asterisk (*) offer instructions on how to make optical toys and gadgets such as pinhole cameras, flip books, and thaumatropes.

PRINT

Bankston, John. *Story of the Daguerreotype.* Hockessin, Del.: Mitchell Lane Publishers, 2004.

Barnouw, Erik. *The Magician and the Cinema.* New York: Oxford University Press, 1981.

Bohn, Thomas W., and Richard L. Stromgren. *Light and Shadows: A History of Motion Pictures.* Mountain View, Calif.: Mayfield Publishing Company, 1975.

Braun, Marta. *Picturing Time: The Work of Etienne-Jules Marey (1830–1904).* Chicago: University of Chicago Press, 1992.

Ceram, C. W. *Archaeology of the Cinema.* New York: Harcourt, Brace & World, 1965.

Cheshire, David F. *The Book of Movie Photography.* New York: Alfred A. Knopf, 1979.

*Churchill, E. Richard. *How to Make Optical Illusion Tricks and Toys.* New York: Sterling Publishing Co., ca. 1989.

Coe, Brian. *The History of Movie Photography.* London: Ash & Grant, 1981.

Comment, Bernard. *The Painted Panorama.* New York: Harry N. Abrams, 2000.

Gernsheim, Helmut. *L.J.M. Daguerre: The History of the Diorama and the Daguerreotype.* New York: Dover Publications, 1968.

Haas, Robert Bartlett. *Muybridge: Man in Motion.* Berkeley: University of California Press, 1976.

Hammond, John H. *The Camera Obscura/A Chronicle.* Bristol, U.K.: Adam Hilger Limited, 1981.

Hendricks, Gordon. *Eadweard Muybridge: The Father of the Motion Picture.* New York: Dover Publications, 2001.

——. *The Edison Motion Picture Myth.* Berkeley: University of California Press, 1967.

——. *Origins of the American Film.* New York: Arno Press, 1972.

*Jenkins, Patrick. *Flipbook Animation and Other Ways to Make Cartoons Move.* Toronto: Kids Can Press, 1991.

Kukes, Roger, *The Zoetrope Book,* 2nd ed. Portland, Ore.: Klassroom Kinetics, 1989.

Mannoni, Laurent. *The Great Art of Light and Shadow: Archaeology of the Cinema.* Exeter, U.K.: University of Exeter Press, 2000.

Mast, Gerald. *A Short History of the Movies,* 2nd ed. Indianapolis: Bobbs-Merrill, 1976.

Musser, Charles. *The Emergence of Cinema: The American Screen to 1907.* New York: Charles Scribner's Sons, 1990.

———. *Thomas A. Edison and His Kinetographic Motion Pictures.* New Brunswick, N.J.: Rutgers University Press, 1995.

Newhall, Beaumont. *The History of Photography, from 1839 to the Present Day.* New York: The Museum of Modern Art, 1964.

Quigley, Martin. *Magic Shadows: The Story of the Origin of Motion Pictures.* New York: Biblo and Tannen, 1969.

Rhode, Eric. *A History of the Cinema from Its Origins to 1970.* New York: Hill and Wang, 1976.

Robinson, David. *From Peep Show to Palace: The Birth of American Film.* New York: Columbia University Press, ca. 1996.

———. *The History of World Cinema.* New York: Stein and Day, 1973.

———. *The Lantern Image: Iconography of the Magic Lantern.* London: Magic Lantern Society, 1993.

Rossell, Deac. *Living Pictures: The Origins of the Movies.* Albany, N.Y.: SUNY Press, 1998.

Sacks, Oliver. *Uncle Tungsten: Memories of a Chemical Boyhood.* New York: Alfred A. Knopf, 2001.

Sipley, Louis Walton. "The Magic Lantern." *Pennsylvania Arts and Sciences,* volume 4 (December 1939): 39–43.

Spehr, Paul C. *The Movies Begin: Making Movies in New Jersey, 1887–1920.* Newark: The Newark Museum, 1977.

Warner, Marina, et al. *Tony Oursler: The Influence Machine.* London: Artangel, in association with the Public Art Fund, New York, 2002.

Williams, Christopher, ed. *Cinema: the Beginnings and the Future*. London: University of Westminster Press, 1996.

VIDEO

The Magic of Méliès. Dir. Jacques Meny, 1997. From the DVD *Méliès the Magician*. Chicago: Facets Video, 2001.

WEBSITES

Adventures in Cybersound. A comprehensive collection of information on pre-cinema history. Dr. Russell Naughton has collected and assembled information from a variety of sources and arranged it chronologically. The site is now permanently archived as part of the National Library of Australia's Pandora Project. It can be somewhat confusing and difficult to navigate at times, but it is unequaled for the amount of information it contains. www.acmi.net.au/AIC

The American Magic Lantern Theater. This a contemporary company that puts on magic lantern shows all across the United States. Their site contains information about the company, their shows, and bookings, as well as a short history of the magic lantern and other interesting tidbits. www.magiclanternshows.com

The Athanasius Kircher Project at Stanford University. This is a fine collection of information about Kircher, including his correspondence and images of many of his inventions. http://kircher.stanford.edu

The Bill Douglas Centre for the History of Cinema and Popular Culture. This site, from the University of Exeter in Britain, has a large collection of images, and special educational features designed for young people. In addition to the collections database, there are virtual exhibitions of the panorama, magic lantern, and optical toys. There is also a section called "Young BDC," which has a number of interesting exhibits, including "Behind the Scenes" (a history of cinema), a tour of the collections, and an invitation to e-mail the staff with questions. www.ex.ac.uk/bill.douglas

The California Museum of Photography (University of California/Riverside). The Eadweard Muybridge exhibit at this museum features one hundred of Muybridge's motion studies, animated. www.photo.ucr.edu/photographers/muybridge

CineScene. This is a website that describes itself as "by and for movie lovers." It consists of movie reviews and articles on a wide range of cinematic topics. The site is edited by Chris Dashiell. www.cinescene.com

*Chronophotographical Projections. From the Netherlands (but available in English) comes this excellent site by Charl Lucassen. There are descriptive articles on many of the people discussed in this book—and more. There is also a section on optical toys (thaumatropes, zoetropes, etc.) that has animated illustrations. (The zoetrope section has a link to a site with instructions on how to build your own zoetrope.) http://web.inter.nl.net/users/anima/pre-cinema/index.htm

The Complete History of the Discovery of Cinematography. The title of this site says it all. It's a chronological history of the moving image from 900 B.C. to A.D. 1900. Developed and maintained by Paul T. Burns, it is packed with information and illustrations. www.precinemahistory.net

The Dead Media Project. This is a hard-to-describe site comprised of notes on all kinds of media that are no longer functional in our digital age—that is, most of the media in this book. According to the website, "The Dead Media Project consists of a database of field notes written and researched by members of the Project's mailing list." You won't find a well-organized presentation of information here, but you will find lots of interesting bits and pieces. The site is the brainchild of Bruce Sterling, writer, critic, editor, and professor of International Studies and Science Fiction at the European Graduate School, Saas-Fe, Switzerland. From the home page, go to "dead media working notes," then to "categorical listings." www.deadmedia.org

de Luikerwaal (Dutch Magic Lantern). *Luikerwallen* is the name for people from Wallonia in Belgium. They were originally rat exterminators, but the government forbade them from carrying rat poison throughout the country, so they sought another livelihood. They became traveling magic lanternists. This site has very good sections on all kinds of things to do with magic lanterns, along with excellent illustrations of lanterns, slides, and various curiosities. When you first log on, you'll see that the site is written in Dutch. Click on "English" in the upper left-hand corner. www.luikerwaal.com

Early Cinema. This site includes a timeline of early cinema history (1827–1905); an alphabetical quick reference index to various topics and personalities; essays; and links to other resources. www.earlycinema.com

Early Visual Media. An extensive collection of text and pictures on early photography, pre-cinema, and film, with one of the best collections of slides and equipment from the phantasmagoria. This site is an ongoing project created by the Belgian photographer and media historian Thomas Weynants. www.visual-media.be

*****Eastman Kodak.** One of the best-known makers of photographic equipment offers instructions for making your own pinhole camera using common household materials. www.kodak.com/global/en/consumer/education/lessonPlans/pinholeCamera

Etienne-Jules Marey: Movement in Light. A virtual exhibition of Marey's life and work with very good examples of his photographs, equipment, and more. The exhibit is curated by the French scholar Laurent Mannoni, author, curator of equipment collections at Cinémathèque Française and Centre National de la Cinématographie, and member of the National Panel of Specialist Experts. www.expo-marey.com/anglais/home.html

Galante So. Magic lantern slides, old photographs, and obscure information on a variety of nineteenth-century subjects. www.jhenry.demon.co.uk/galantee.htm

Glass Harmonicas. At the website of G. Finkenbeiner Inc., manufacturers of glass products, you will find harmonicas much like the ones Robertson used in his phantasmagoria. Not only can you see the harmonicas, but you can also hear them. MP3 sound samples are available. www.finkenbeiner.com/GLASSHARMONICA.htm

At the website of Thomas Bloch, a rare-instrument musician who plays the glass harmonica, you will find information about the harmonica and a repertoire of music composed for it. www.chez.com/thomasbloch/engGLASS.htm

A History of Photography. As its creator, Dr. Robert Leggat, describes this website, it is "a hypertext history of photography covering all major people and processes from the earliest days up to the 1920s." Dr. Leggat is a highly regarded teacher and author, and is a member of Britain's Royal Photographic Society. www.rleggat.com/photohistory.

Laura Hayes and John Howard Wileman Exhibit of Optical Toys. Toy lanterns, zoetropes, praxinoscopes, thaumatropes—this site has them all. This collection of pre-twentieth-century optical toys was donated to the North Carolina School of Science and Mathematics by Dr. Ralph Wileman. For each toy there is a short article about its history and how it works, along with links to animations, videos, and other resources. http://courses.ncssm.edu/gallery/collections/toys/opticaltoys.htm

The Library of Congress American Memory Collections, "America's First Look into the Camera: Daguerreotype Portraits and Views, 1839–1864." This collection consists of more than 725 American daguerreotypes, an explanation of the daguerreotype process and equipment, and a timeline of the period. http://memory.loc.gov/ammem/daghtml/daghome.html

The Library of Congress American Memory Collections, "Inventing Entertainment: The Early Motion Pictures and Sound Recordings of the Edison Companies." This collection contains a wealth of information about the contributions of Edison and his associates to the development of movies, and also contains videos of many of the films produced by the Edison Companies. http://memory.loc.gov/ammem/edhtml/edhome.html

The Magic Lantern Society. Features animated magic lantern slides of various types. www.magiclantern.org.uk/animations.htm

The Magic Mirror of Life. Contains everything you want to know about the camera obscura. Jack and Beverly Wilgus feature examples of camera obscuras from their own extensive collection, pictures of camera obscura rooms in the U.S. and Europe, and a bibliography and links to additional information. http://brightbytes.com/cosite/cohome.html

The Material History of American Religion Project. Based at the Divinity School at Vanderbilt University, this project set out to study American religion by focusing on material objects and economic themes. It was conducted by a team of scholars led by James Hudnut-Beumler, dean of the Divinity School. The project is now completed. The article from *Church History* referred to in the Source Notes is one of hundreds of documents collected for the project. www.materialreligion.org.

Midley History of Photography. The website contains a collection of academic research articles on the history of photography by the British scholar R. Derek Wood, written between 1970 and 1997. www.midleykent.fsnet.co.uk.

The Missing Link. This is a British site devoted to the horror films of the 1920s, 1930s, and 1940s. It contains reviews of films and information about the people who made and acted in them. www.mshepley.btinternet.co.uk.

The Museum of the Moving Image (MOMI). Enter the Optical Room at this British virtual museum and tour fascinating exhibits about most of the visual media mentioned in this book. Some illustrations are animated. The site is developed and maintained by Stephen Herbert. http://easyweb.easynet.co.uk/~s-herbert/momiwelcome.htm

*****Old Sturbridge Village.** The website of Old Sturbridge Village, Massachussetts, offers kid-friendly instructions for making a thaumatrope, the simplest persistence of vision toy. www.osv.org/kids/crafts7.htm

Phi Phenomenon (persistence of vision). From Canada's York University comes this entertaining site with an animation illustrating how persistence of vision works. There are also a number of other topics having to do with optical illusions and perception. www.yorku.ca/eye/balls.htm

Projectors and Slides. A nice display of magic lantern projectors and slides from Thomas B. Greenslade Jr. of the physics department at Kenyon College. Good illustrations of some mechanical slides, showing how they work. Browse the site for other interesting scientific instruments. http://physics.kenyon.edu/EarlyApparatus/Optics/Projector/Projector.html

*Public Broadcasting System. The PBSKids website offers printable activity pages with instructions for making several of the optical toys discussed in this book. http://pbskids.org/zoom/printables/index.html

The Victorian Dictionary. This site collects nineteenth-century texts, photographs, articles, advertisements, and so on—anything to do with life in London during the Victorian Age. Examples of topics: photography and optical, entertainment and recreation, childhood, science and technology. The site's creator, Lee Jackson, is a librarian at the University of East London and a writer of several novels set in Victorian times. www.victorianlondon.org

The Victorian Magic Lantern (The Randall-Salter Collection). Great examples of animated magic lantern slides. www/poppyland.co.uk/lantern

Victorian Station. Timeline of important events (mostly in the United States and Britain) from 1820 to 1900. Check the home page for all kinds of information on matters Victorian. www.victorianstation.com/timelinefull.htm

Who's Who of Victorian Cinema. This website is a revised and expanded version of the book of the same title published by the British Film Institute in 1996. It boasts an impressive list of twenty-seven contributors, selected for their expertise in various aspects of cinema history. The bulk of the site consists of biographical essays about prominent and not-so-prominent figures in the history of cinema, and it also contains a good deal of technical information. www.victorian-cinema.net

*Worldwide Pinhole Photography Day. Worldwide Pinhole Day is an international event created to promote and celebrate the art of pinhole photography. This site has instructions for making and using pinhole cameras under its "Resources" section and offers a gallery of photographs taken with pinhole cameras. www.pinholeday.org

Index

Note: Page numbers in **bold** type refer to illustrations.